HOMEPLACE

Sarah Christianson

Introduction by Arnold R. Alanen

Daylight

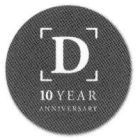

Daylight

Editors: Taj Forer and Michael Itkoff
Design: Ursula Damm
Copyediting: Dianne Timblin

Excerpt from *The Lure of the Local: Senses of Place in a Multicentered Society,* © 1998 by Lucy Lippard.
Reprinted by permission of The New Press. www.thenewpress.com

ISBN 978-0-9832316-9-1

Printed in China

Cover image: Entryway, Christianson farm, 2008

Daylight Books
E-mail: info@daylightbooks.org
Web: www.daylightbooks.org

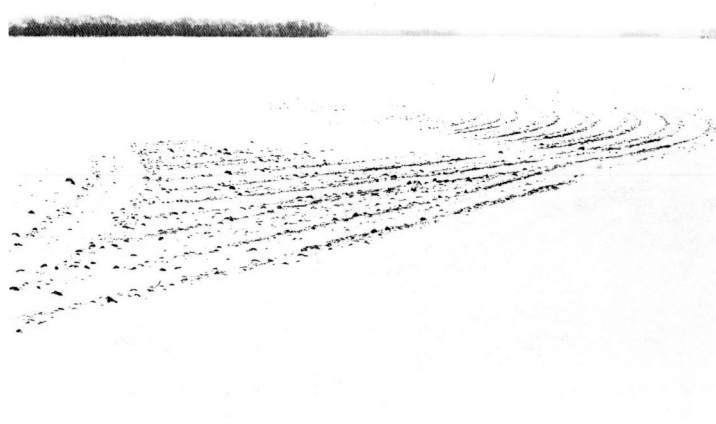

East of house, 2007

The search for homeplace is the mythical search
for the axis mundi, for a center, for some place to stand,
for something to hang on to.

—Lucy Lippard, *The Lure of the Local*

INTRODUCTION

Norway to North Dakota: A Christianson Family Saga

Arnold R. Alanen, Professor Emeritus
University of Wisconsin–Madison

In 1869 twenty-four-year-old Hans Olai Cornelius Christianson (see page 10) immigrated to Minnesota from Bodø, a community located along the rugged northern coastline of Norway. Christianson (1845–1927) was one of at least 800,000 émigrés who, over the span of a century (1825–1925), departed Norway to pursue a life in the United States. Overall, these emigrants represented one-third of Norway's total population—a figure exceeded only by Ireland.[1]

Norwegians settled throughout the United States, but a majority made their way to the Midwest. By 1910, the four states with the largest concentrations of Norwegian immigrants were located in the nation's heartland: Minnesota (103,505), Wisconsin (57,000), North Dakota (45,935), and Illinois (32,915). No state, however, had a higher proportion of Norwegians in its population than North Dakota: 32 percent of the state's foreign-born residents were natives of Norway in 1910. Today, when just 1.5 percent of the nation's population claims some Norwegian ancestry, the North Dakota figure stands at an astounding 31 percent. Similarly, North Dakota has the three most Norwegian counties in the entire United States: Divide (65 percent), Steele (62 percent), and Traill (59 percent).[2]

Christianson settled in Minneapolis, where in 1873 he married Martha Ellingrud (1844–1927), also an 1869 immigrant. In 1878 the Christianson family—which by that time included two children, Christian and Martin—participated in the Norwegian diaspora to North Dakota, where they established a homestead sixteen miles (twenty-five kilometers) west of the Red River, about equidistant between Fargo and Grand Forks. The initial movement of Norwegians to the Red River area began in 1859 when land was opened for settlement, but large-scale settlement did not commence until 1869.[3]

The Red River (also called the Red River of the North) is distinctive for its remarkably flat basin, or watershed, that 9,500 years ago was filled with the water of glacial Lake Agassiz. Although the shallow valley formed by the river is only some hundreds of feet wide, the term *Red River Valley* is commonly used when referring to a larger section of the basin or Lake Agassiz Plain. Over time an extensive system of ditches and culverts was developed to drain seasonal standing water into streams and holding ponds. The Red River has a very slight gradient of only one foot per mile (one meter per five kilometers) from its source at Breckenridge, Minnesota, to the U.S.-Manitoba border. Since the entire river runs 550 miles (885 kilometers) northward from Breckenridge until it drains into Lake Winnipeg, the water produced by early snowmelts in the warmer southern sections of the basin sometimes encounters ice dams that impede the outflow. This phenomenon can result in major floods that are exacerbated by the terrain—one of the flattest areas in North America. As the flood spreads over the basin, fields, farmsteads, roads, towns, and cities are inundated with water.[4] Despite the natural hazards that Red River Valley denizens may encounter—not only floods, but also droughts, tornadoes, and blizzards—the organically rich Boroll soils that formed at the bottom of Lake Agassiz have been profitable for farmers since the 1860s.

Quite obviously, the Christiansons and tens of thousands of other Norwegians who settled in the Red River Valley and across the entirety of North Dakota were not searching for a physical environment that reminded them of their homeland. Instead, the settlement decisions of most immigrants were driven by economic concerns. Christianson and his compatriots recognized that "if one wanted free land with the potential of reasonable agricultural production, [then] there was no other place to go." By the late nineteenth century North Dakota represented "the farmer's last frontier."[5]

When Olai Christianson applied for a homestead in 1878, he also filed a "declaration of intention" to become a United States citizen, a necessary step for any immigrant hoping to acquire a homestead. The Christiansons' 160-acre (65 hectare) Traill County claim was located in the southeastern quarter of Section 6 in East Blanchard (later Bloomfield) Township (see page 26). During the summer of 1878 Christianson built a 14 x 16 foot log house that had three windows, a board floor, and a shingled roof. (Anecdotal information indicates that Christianson may have resided in a dugout in a coulee bank while he was building the house.) The family established permanent residence on the property in early November of 1878. Christianson became a citizen in 1883, and in November of that year he and two neighbors gave testimony regarding his accomplishments, all achieved over the previous five years: the construction of two additional buildings (a 12 x 14 foot granary and a 14 x 24 foot straw stable), the "breaking" of one hundred acres (40 hectares) of land, and the raising of crops during each year. The estimated value of the entire holding, including land and buildings, was $1,100. President Chester A. Arthur signed the Christiansons' official homestead certificate on October 4, 1884 (see page 27). Three more children—Clara, Nellie, and Andrew—arrived between 1879 and 1890.[6]

The Christiansons and other homesteaders were not alone in their quest to acquire land and establish farms in the Red River Valley of North Dakota and Minnesota. Also emerging simultaneously were the valley's "bonanza farms"—America's first gigantic agricultural ventures. These farms were spawned after the Panic of 1873, which resulted in bankruptcy for the Northern Pacific Railway Company and the loss of its huge land holdings. The company's properties were quickly snapped up at very low prices by eastern capitalists who "applied business practices to agriculture . . . [and] secured large blocks of land, professional management, and large-scale machinery to create the bonanza farms." At least ninety such farms, each with more than 3,000 acres (1,215 hectares), were formed before the 1920s; the largest, owned by the Dalrymple family, produced wheat on most of its 28,000 acres (11,330 hectares) in 1888. Traill County included at least five bonanzas; one, the Blanchard farm, was located just west of the Christianson homestead.[7]

Bonanza farms thrived when weather and economic circumstances were favorable, but experienced severe problems when uncertainty or challenging conditions arose; most farms had already been disbanded or were in decline by the time a post–World War I agricultural depression impacted much of rural America. Smaller farms with their operational success based on the labor and contributions of family members, however, were much better equipped to survive such difficult situations. The Christiansons' early twentieth-century history is indicative of the procedures that families used to expand their farms and transfer them to subsequent generations. The first expansion occurred sometime before 1909 when Olai purchased an additional 160 acres of land in Section 5 that adjoined the homestead. In 1910 the U.S. Census reported that Olai and Martha, then approaching their mid-60s, had retired; the farm was now operated by two sons: Martin, a thirty-three-year-old widower with a two-year-old daughter, and twenty-year-old Andrew. When Martin married again, this time to a Norwegian

Grandpa Everett combining wheat, 1941

immigrant, he settled nearby on his own 160-acre tract. Andrew, his wife Mabel (born in Canada), and their five children remained on the original place. After the death of both his parents in 1927, Andrew bought out the other Christianson siblings and became the sole owner of the farm, which now included 320 acres (130 hectares).[8] As will be seen in this discussion, further expansions and transfers of farms and farmland remained a consistent thread in the lives of later Christianson generations.

The bonanza farms had introduced large-scale machinery such as plows, harrows, seeders, self-binding harvesters ("binders"), and steam threshing rigs to the Red River Valley. Each bonanza farm included large quantities of equipment, as well as hundreds of horses to tow them. In fact, the most iconic images of bonanza farming depict scores of horses pulling seeders, binders, or grain wagons across a seemingly endless horizon. Steam-powered tractors were also used for plowing, but it was not until World War I, during the final years of the bonanza period, that gasoline tractors appeared in noticeable numbers. As early as 1919 federal agricultural specialists were encouraging North and South Dakota farmers to utilize gasoline tractors; soon the valley's "typical" farmers would lead the nation in adopting much of the new technology. Indeed, the Christiansons had replaced all of their horses with tractors by the early 1930s.[9]

Wheat served as the Christiansons' primary agricultural product and source of income, but they also raised barley, oats, and a few other cash crops. Until the mid-twentieth century the farm also included a few dairy cows, beef cattle, pigs, and chickens that supplied food for the family. Andrew and Mabel's youngest son, Everett, ensured that the Christiansons' farming traditions would continue into the twenty-first century. In 1948, Everett married Margaret Anderson—the granddaughter of nineteenth-century Norwegian immigrants Erick and Julia Johnson and Ole and Karoline Anderson. The young couple eventually

settled on the Andersons' Ervin Township farm. With Everett and Margaret's marriage, the farm grew to 960 acres (388 hectares), a combination of Christianson, Anderson, and Johnson lands in the two townships. After the last of the Bloomfield Township farm buildings succumbed to fire, the land was leveled and planted to soybeans (see pages 30–31). Although the buildings are gone, the footprint of the original farmstead is still evident from the air (see page 29). The Ervin Township farmstead was sold to another family in 2006 after Everett's death, but the land remained with the family.[10]

In 1978, Everett and Margaret's son Dale and his wife Rose moved to Margaret's home farm in Ervin Township, which had been purchased by her parents, Henry (Hank) and Claire Anderson in the late 1930s (see pages 36–37). The Christiansons' holdings peaked at 1,280 acres (518 hectares), when two additional quarter sections of land were acquired in the 1950s and 1980s, making the size virtually equivalent to that of an average farm in North Dakota (1,240 acres; 502 hectares) and Traill County (1,182 acres; 478 hectares). While the Christiansons' farm is considerably smaller than most corporate agricultural ventures found throughout the state, its acreage is adequate to function as a profitable family-run unit. All labor required to plant and harvest the farm's primary crops—wheat and soybeans, along with some pinto and navy beans occasionally put into the rotation—is provided by Dale and Rose Christianson.[11] This feat, of course, is only possible because of numerous advances in the scale and efficiency of agricultural equipment and technology. Quite appropriately, the origins of these machines and practices may be traced back to the early twentieth-century history of the valley.

None of Dale and Rose Christianson's three children have chosen to continue the family's agrarian traditions. While there apparently will be no fifth generation of farmers, this book, by Olai and Martha Christianson's great-great-granddaughter, Sarah, offers a visual record of the family's 135 years of residence in Traill County.

Appearing throughout the book are Sarah's photographs, along with historical images and documents, all of which reveal change and consistency in local land and life. *Homeplace* portrays generational transitions as Norwegian immigrants and their descendants experience both the mundane and celebratory aspects of life in the Red River Valley. Always present is the landscape, which serves as a stage and backdrop for expanding farming activities. Fields become larger, farm numbers decline, building functions change, and different crops appear, but the geometry and expansiveness of the landscape remain constant—rectangular fields and planting patterns, linear roads and tree windrows, and towns with orthogonal grids. And as Sarah contemplates, with some uncertainty and poignancy, the future of the Christianson family farm in the early twenty-first century and beyond, she finds new meanings and insights after visiting ancestral

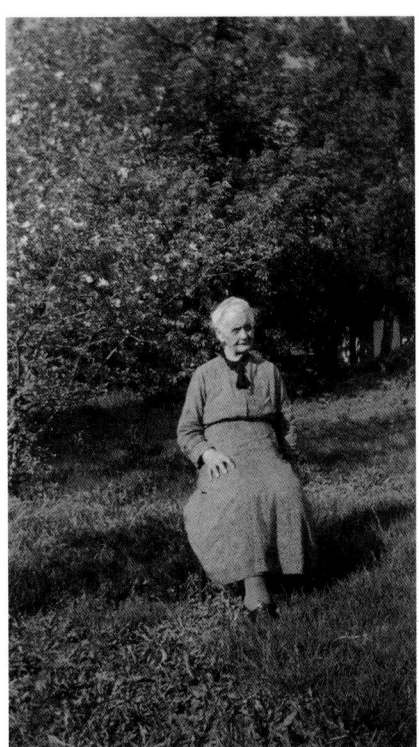 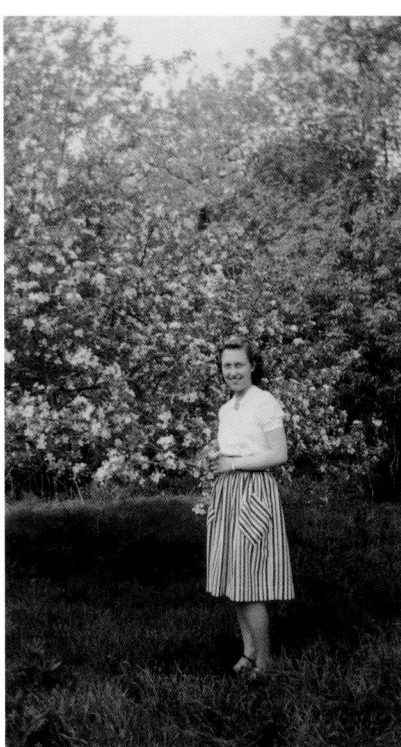 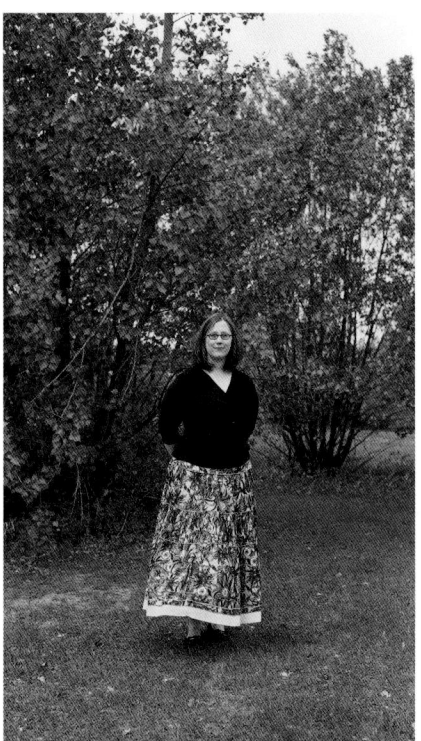

Great-great-grandma Julia, Grandma Margaret, and Sarah

places in Norway. These places, she writes, serve as an "epilogue" for the Christiansons' North Dakota farm.

Clearly, dedication to a common economic pursuit such as farming, when undertaken by several generations of interrelated families in a clearly defined geographic space, represents the work, love, perseverance, pluck, and luck of many people. These situations deserve respect and consideration, something that Sarah clearly demonstrates throughout the pages of *Homeplace*. Other farms and families should be so fortunate.

NOTES

1. Einar Haugan, *The Norwegians in America, 1825–1975* (Oslo: Royal Ministry of Foreign Affairs, 1975), 9–10.

2. William C. Sherman, *Prairie Mosaic: An Ethnic Atlas of Rural North Dakota* (Fargo: North Dakota Center for Regional Studies, 1983), 113–14; Odd S. Lovoll, *The Promise of America: A History of the Norwegian-American People* (Minneapolis: University of Minnesota Press, 1984), 83–85; William C. Sherman and Playford V. Thorson, eds., *Plains Folk: North Dakota's Ethnic History* (Fargo: North Dakota Institute for Regional Studies, 1986), Appendix C; Sogn og Fjordane Fylkeskommune, "Counties with More Than 50% Norwegian Ancestry," data derived from U.S. Census Bureau, American Community Survey, 2009, accessed January 17, 2013, http://www.sf-f.kommune.no/sff/sf-farkiv3.nsf/0/8395D8776DA9AC6AC1257654003E25D9?OpenDocument.

3. Haugan, *Norwegians in America*, 13.

4. John C. Hudson, *Across This Land: A Regional Geography of the United States and Canada* (Baltimore: Johns Hopkins University Press, 2001), 267–69; *Wikipedia*, s.v. "Red River of the North," accessed February 3, 2013, en.wikipedia.org/wiki/Red_River_of_the_North.

5. D. Jerome Tweton, "The Norwegians in North Dakota History," in *The Way It Was: The North Dakota Frontier Experience. Book Two—Norwegian Homesteaders*, 2nd ed., eds. Everett C. Albers and D. Jerome Tweton (Fessenden, ND: Grass Roots Press, 2001), viii. North and South Dakota became separate states in 1889.

6. Hans Olai Christianson homestead application 6870, Fargo Land Office, 1883 proof, National Archives and Records Administration, Washington, D.C. The metric dimensions are 4.27 x 4.9 meters for the house; 3.66 x 4.27 meters for the granary; and 4.27 x 7.32 meters for the straw barn.

7. Hiram M. Drache, *The Day of the Bonanza: A History of Bonanza Farming in the Red River Valley of the North* (Fargo: North Dakota Institute for Regional Studies, 1964), 72–73, 78.

8. Drache, *Day of the Bonanza*, 204; U.S. Census Bureau, 1930, 15th census, North Dakota, manuscript, available at archive.org; Communication from Sarah Christianson to author, February 5, 2013. As published census reports include only aggregated data, the only way to gather historical census data about individuals is by using the original unpublished manuscript schedules for 1880, 1900, 1910, 1920, 1930, and 1940. The manuscript schedules are the original forms that census enumerators filled out when securing information about each person in the United States.

9. Drache, *Day of the Bonanza*, 119–20, 204–05; Arnold P. Yerkes and L. M. Church, *The Farm Tractor in the Dakotas*, Farmers' Bulletin 1035 (Washington, D.C.: U.S. Department of Agriculture, 1919), UNT Digital Library, http://digital.library.unt.edu/ark:/67531/metadc96625/; Communication from Sarah Christianson to author, September 24, 2012.

10. Communications from Sarah Christianson to author, February 5 and 7, 2013.

11. Communications from Sarah Christianson to author, June 1, 2012, and February 5, 2013; U.S. Department of Agriculture, Census of Agriculture, 2007, http://www.agcensus.usda.gov/Publications/2007/index.php. Traill County is also a major producer of corn and sugar beets.

Gamle Landet, Old Country

Proving Up

From Tractor to Camera

GAMLE LANDET, OLD COUNTRY

Must he give up the old country, then?

Certainly not, and yet . . . ?

At any rate, he clung to his mates on the prairie, just as much as he did to his mother
and brothers and sisters in the old country . . .

But what about [the farm] in the old country? Who was looking after it now?

—Johan Bojer, *The Emigrants* [1]

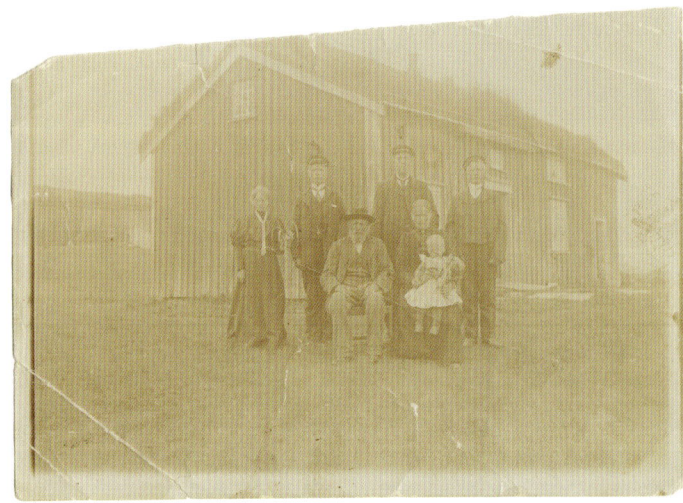

Unidentified family posed in front of house with turf roof, date unknown

The Christianson farm did not start in North Dakota: generations of my family were also farmers in Norway. In the 1870s, six of my great-great-grandparents emigrated from farms scattered across Norway and settled in North Dakota. I wanted to know why they had left and what they had left behind. I already knew they were either unmarried women, husmann (tenant farmers), or younger sons who would not inherit. When they immigrated to the United States, they left Norway, their homes, their extended families, everything they knew. They would never return.

It took a full century to complete the circle. My grandparents reestablished our ties to Norway by conducting extensive genealogical research, contacting distant relatives, and traveling there in 1978 and 1994. I wanted to retrace their steps so I could also inhabit the same places as my ancestors, if just for a moment. I wanted to pick up the threads of their lives and weave a more vivid narrative. My great-great-grandparents left no written accounts of their lives. What we know has been passed down through oral tradition and inferred from research. I wanted to know them on more than just an abstract level. I feel drawn to my ancestors because I also left my home for a different life. I thought that seeing what they saw and learning more about their experiences would inform my own experience.

Most of the farms my ancestors left behind still exist, having been cared for by other families. Only one out of the six, Ellingrud gård, is still owned and operated by a very distant relative, Haakon Jølstad (see pages 8–9); the Jølstads married into the Ellingruds in the 1920s. Two farms near Bodø, above the Arctic Circle—Feneshaugen and Bertnesskeid—were gone entirely (see pages 11, 15). They were absorbed into larger pastures. Few physical traces remained of my ancestors' presence in Norway: a few graves, a letter of recommendation, and the delicate signature of Ole Anderson on a barn wall (see pages 17, 21).

By exploring these origins, I discovered that the beginning is also an epilogue. Others have sustained the farms vacated by my ancestors. Perhaps the Christianson farm in North Dakota will continue in this way and thus bring our agricultural heritage full circle.

1. Johan Bojer, *The Emigrants*, trans. A. G. Jayne (St. Paul: Minnesota Historical Society Press, 1991), 206–228.

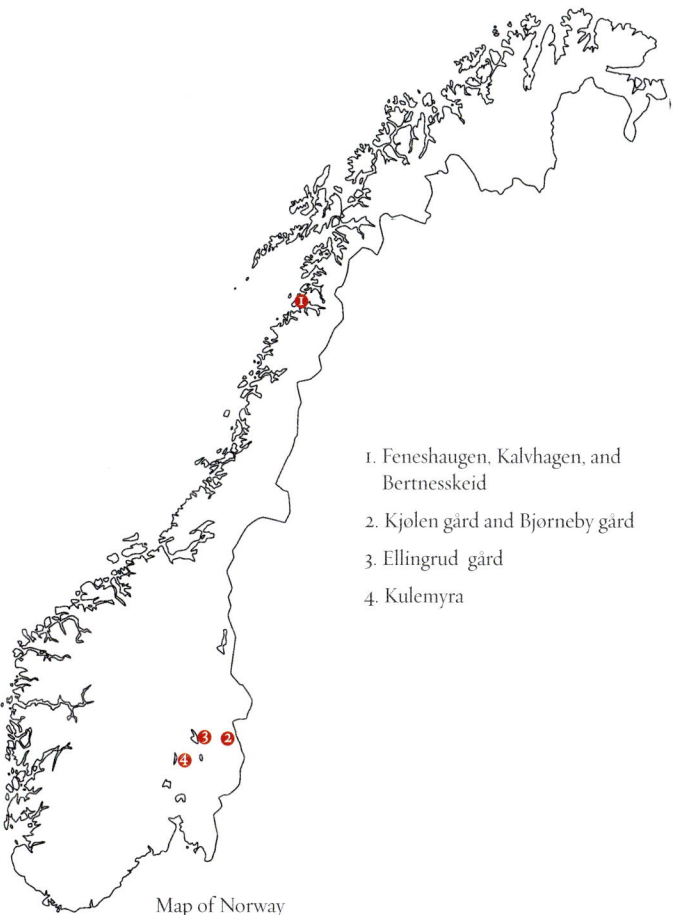

1. Feneshaugen, Kalvhagen, and Bertnesskeid

2. Kjølen gård and Bjørneby gård

3. Ellingrud gård

4. Kulemyra

Map of Norway

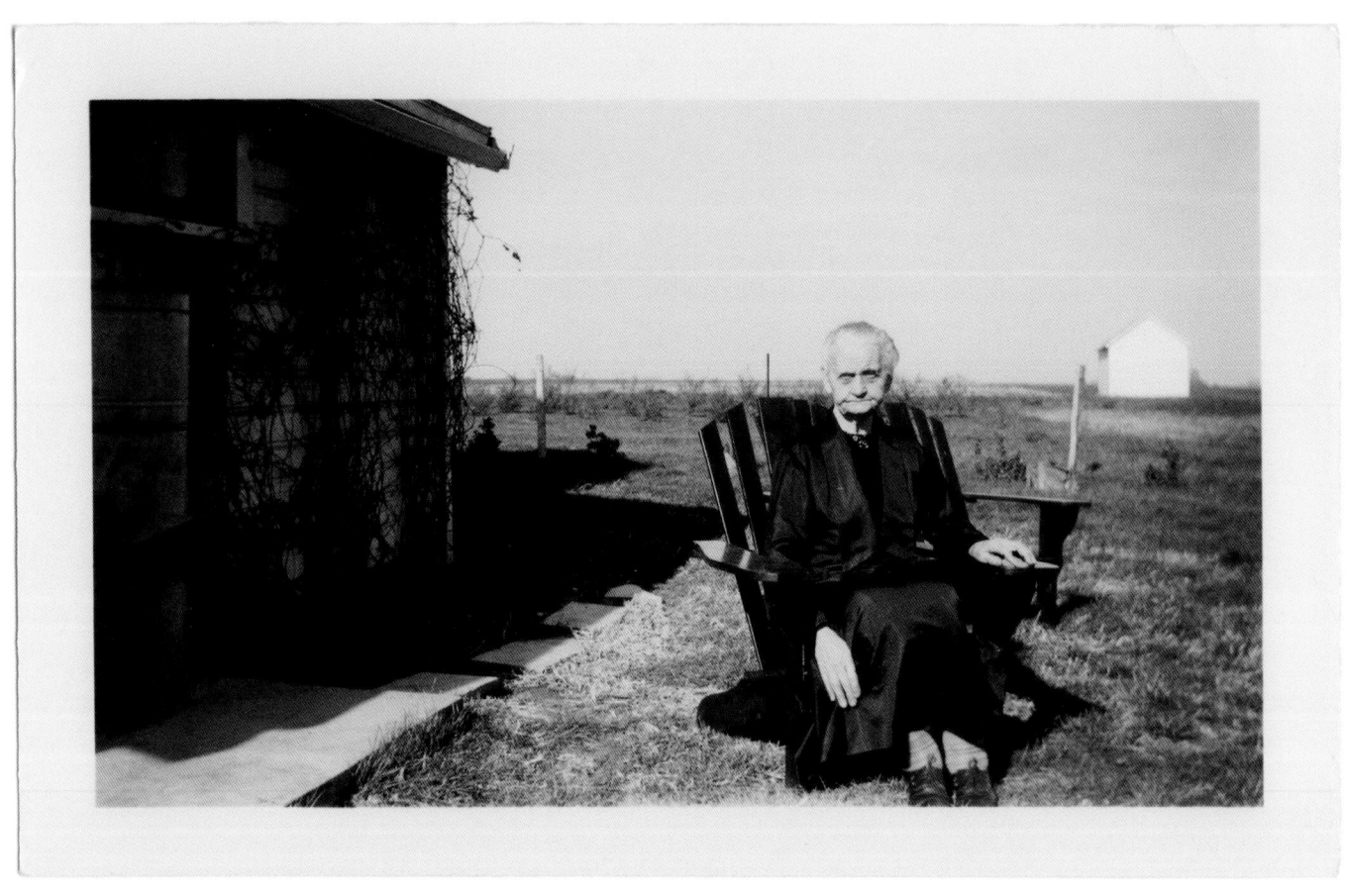

Julia Olson Johnson, c. 1940s

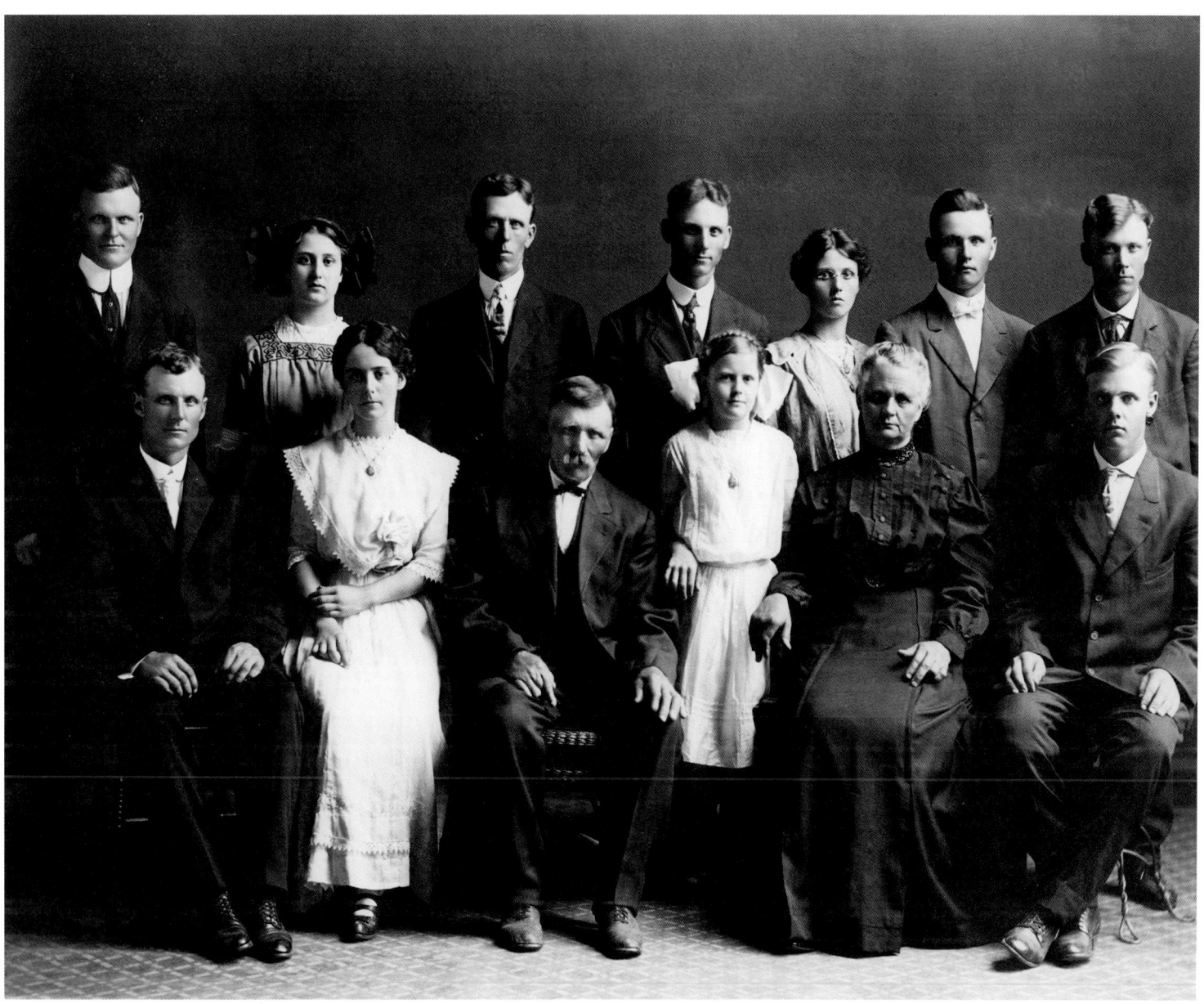

Erick and Julia Olson Johnson and their 11 children, c. 1912

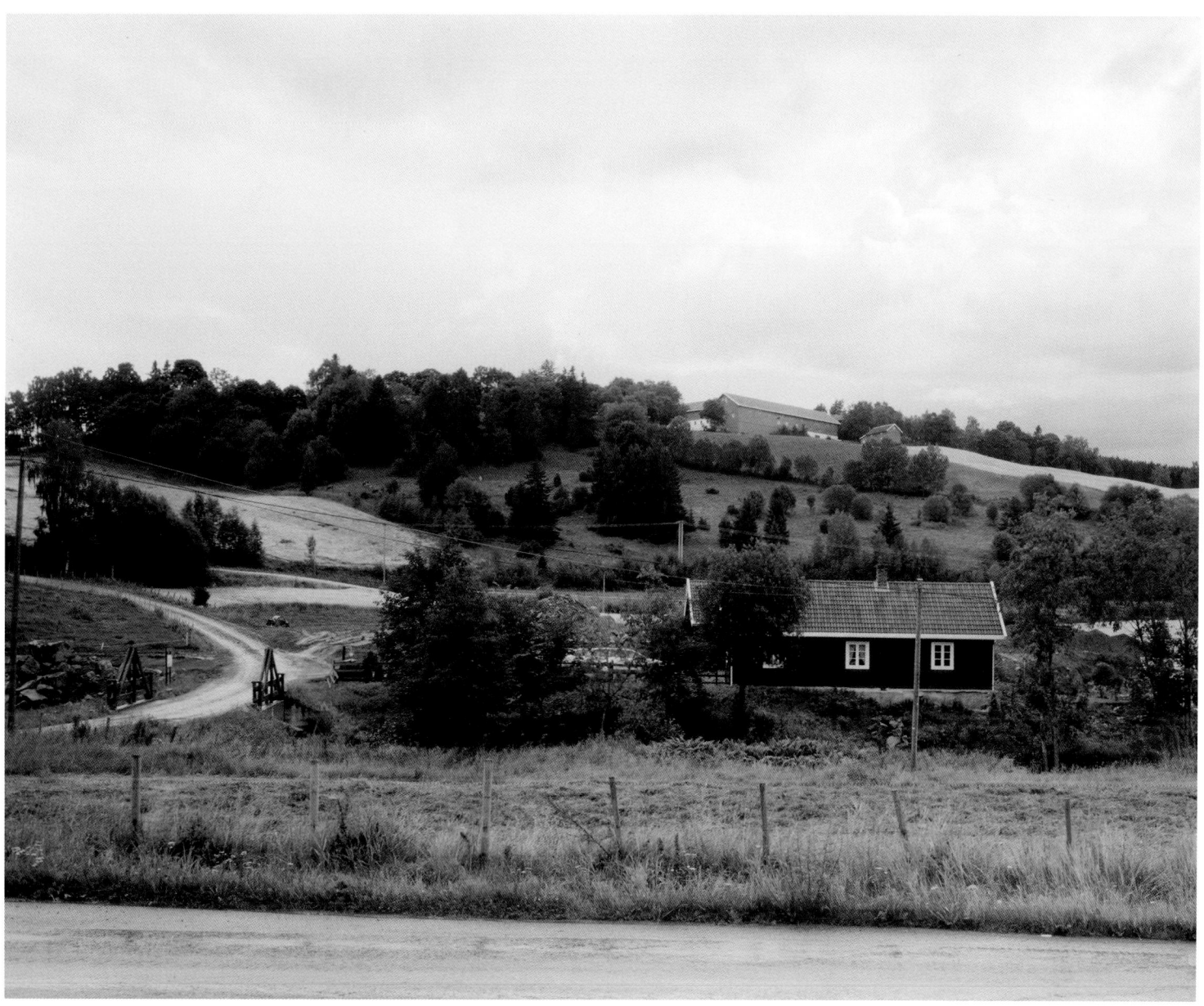

Kulemyra below Dvergsten gård, 2008

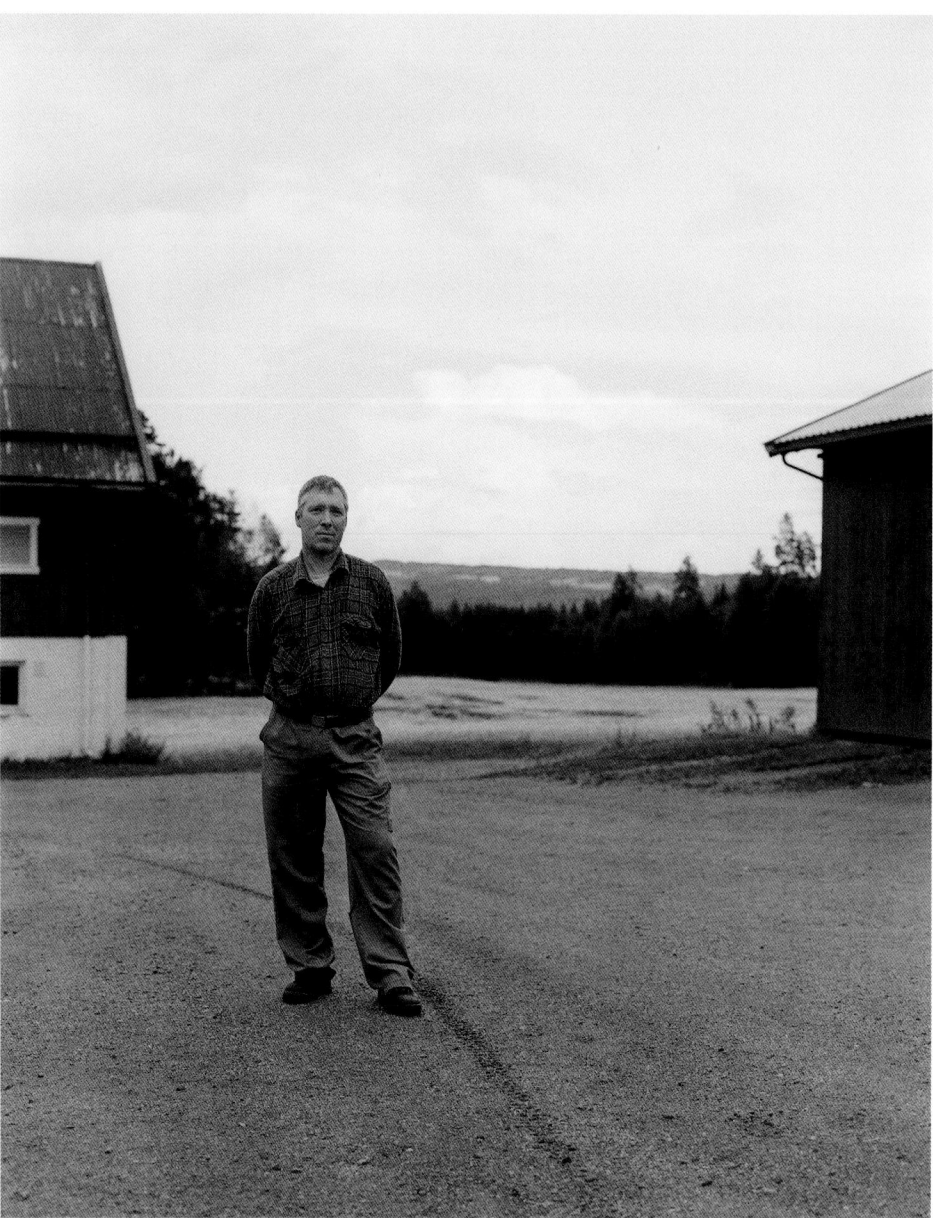

Haakon Jølstad, 2008

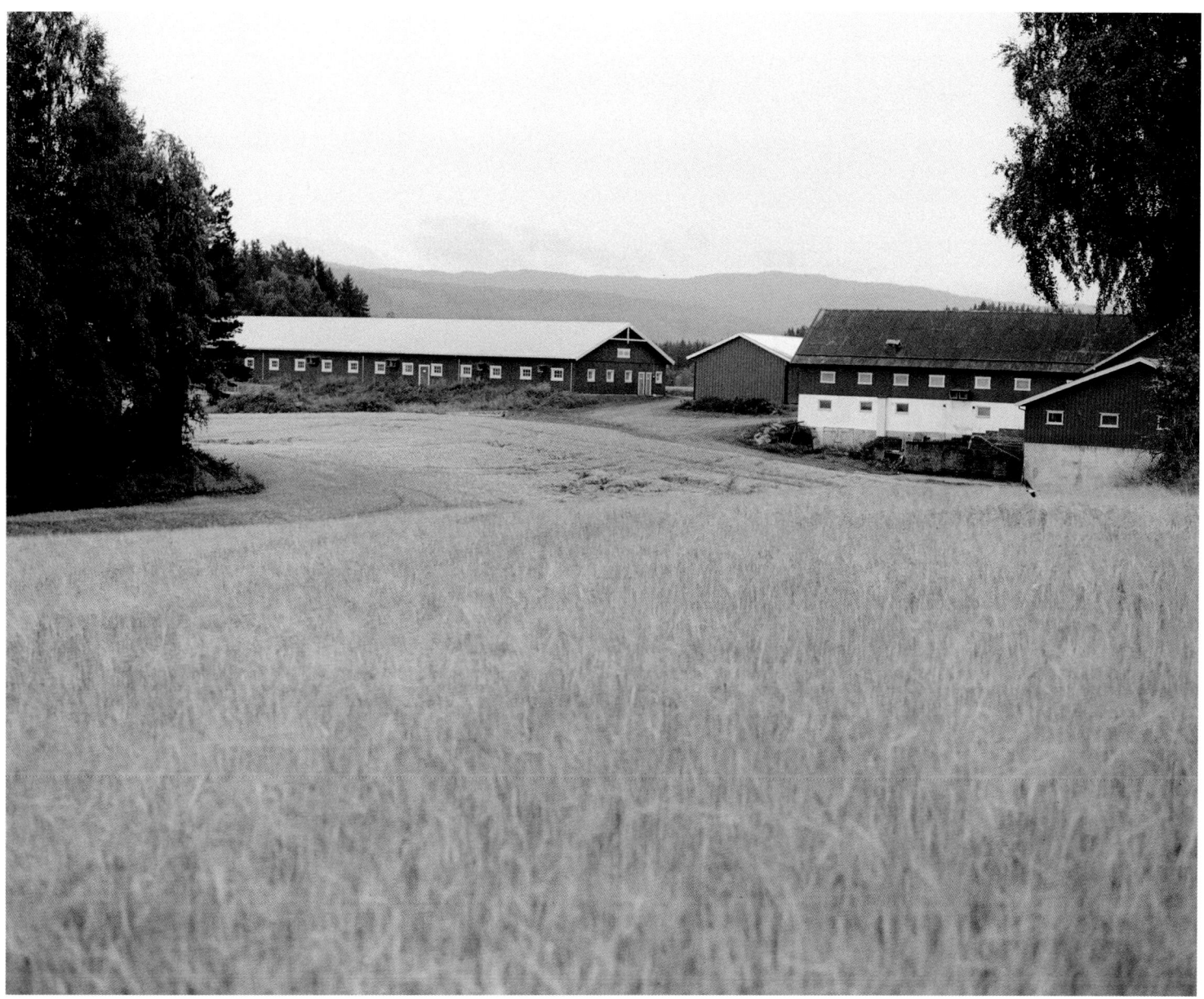

Ellingrud gård, 2008

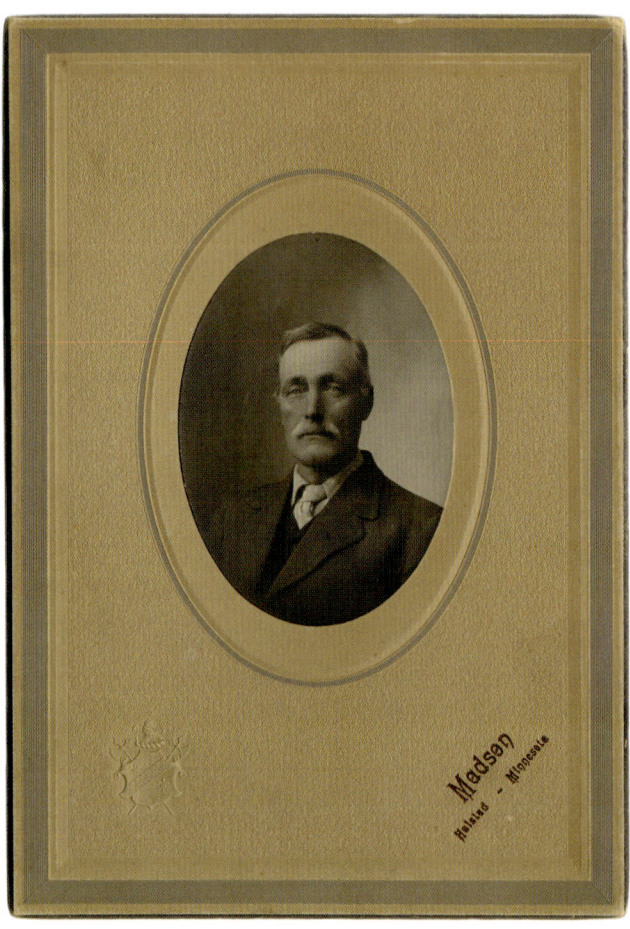

Hans Olai Cornelius Christianson, c. 1910s

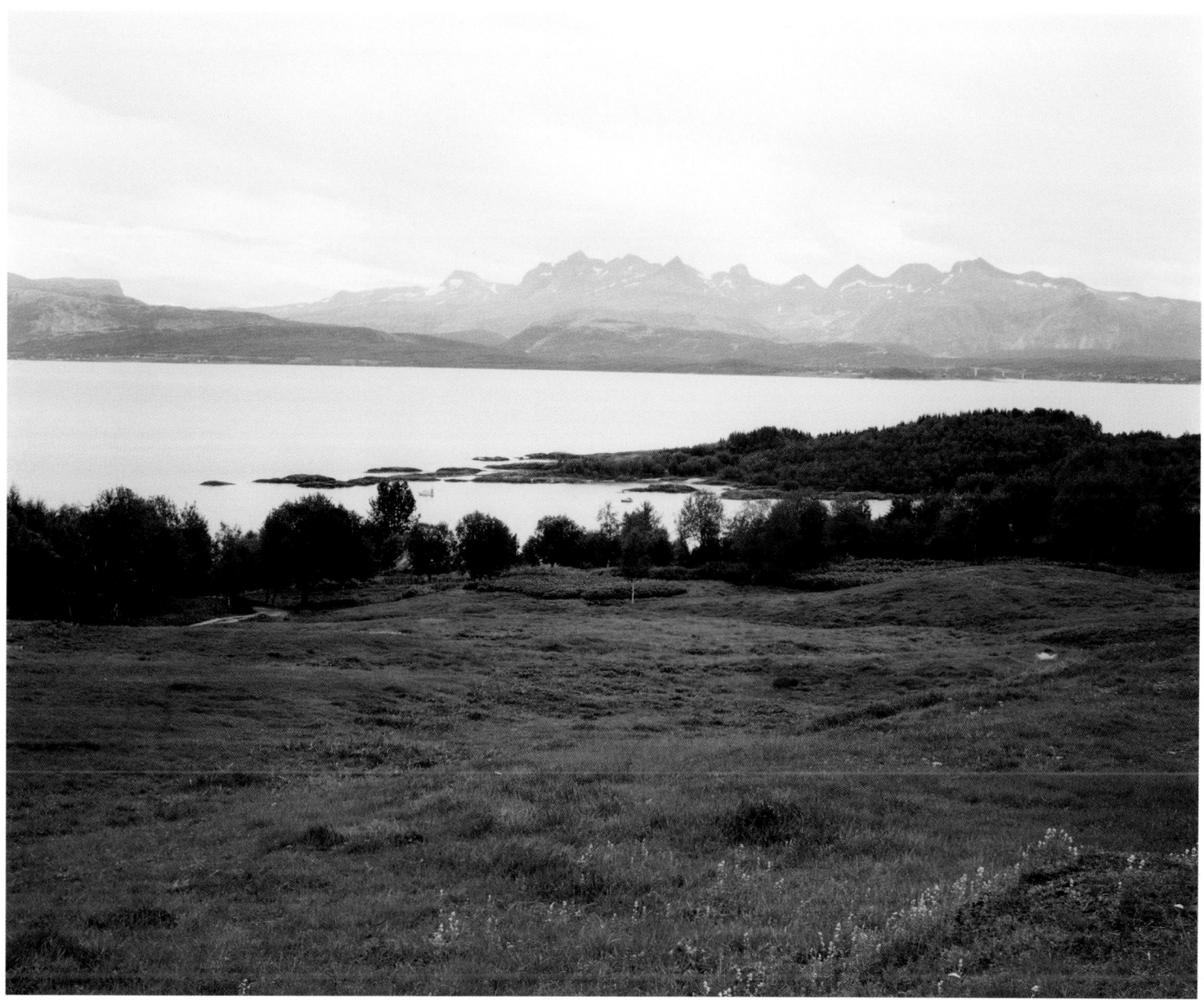

Feneshaugen, 2008

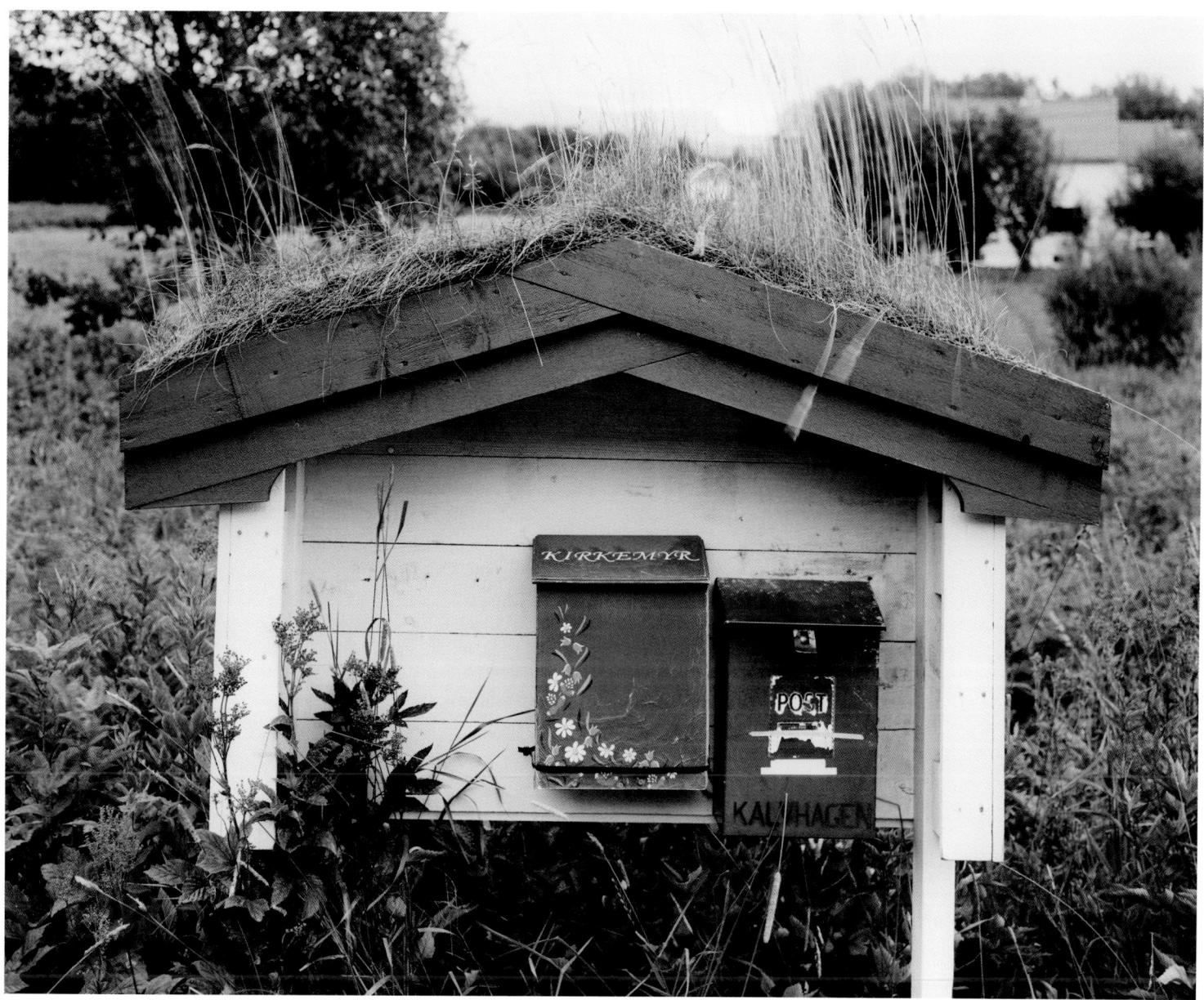

Kalvhagen, 2008

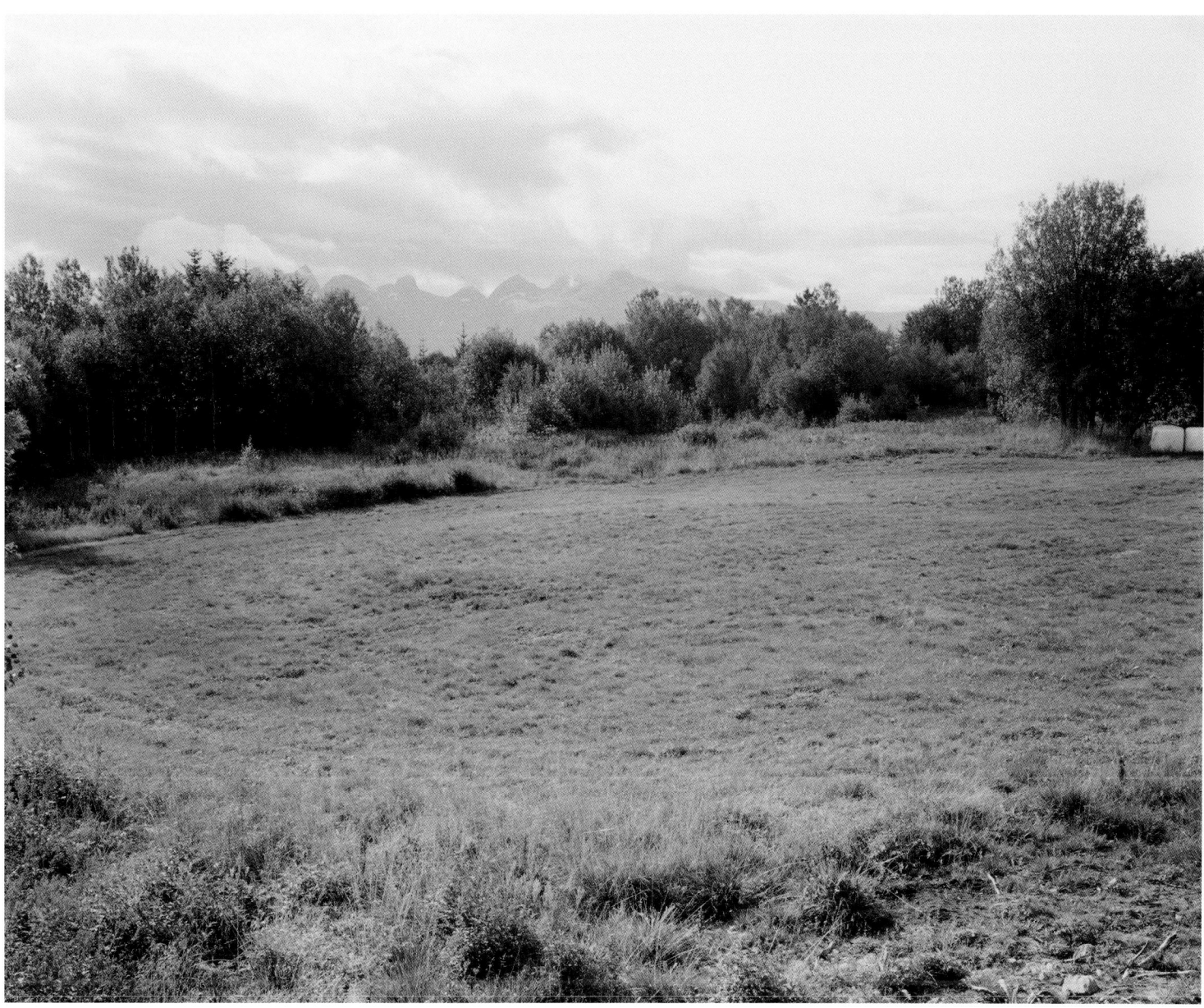

Bertnesskeid, 2008

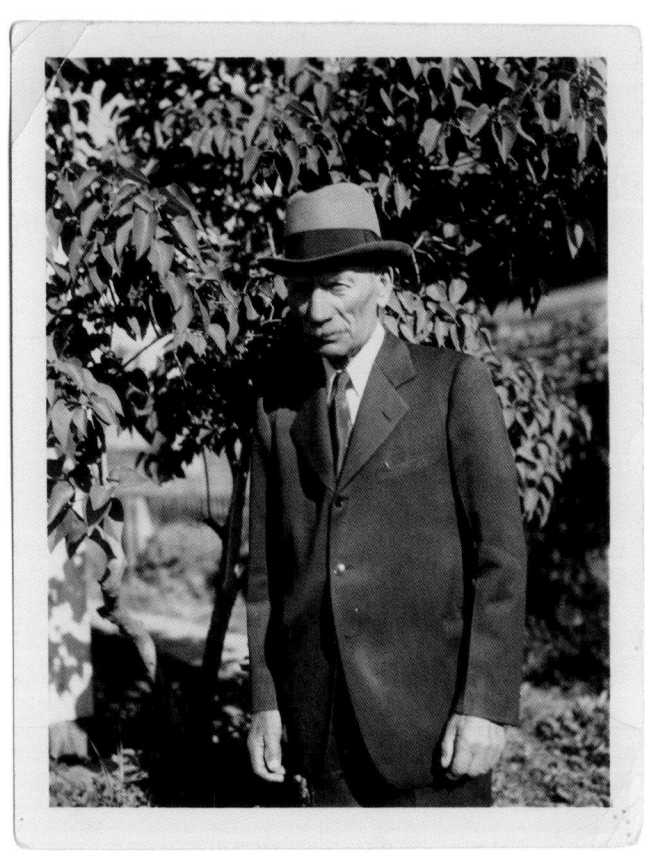

Ole Anderson, c. 1940s

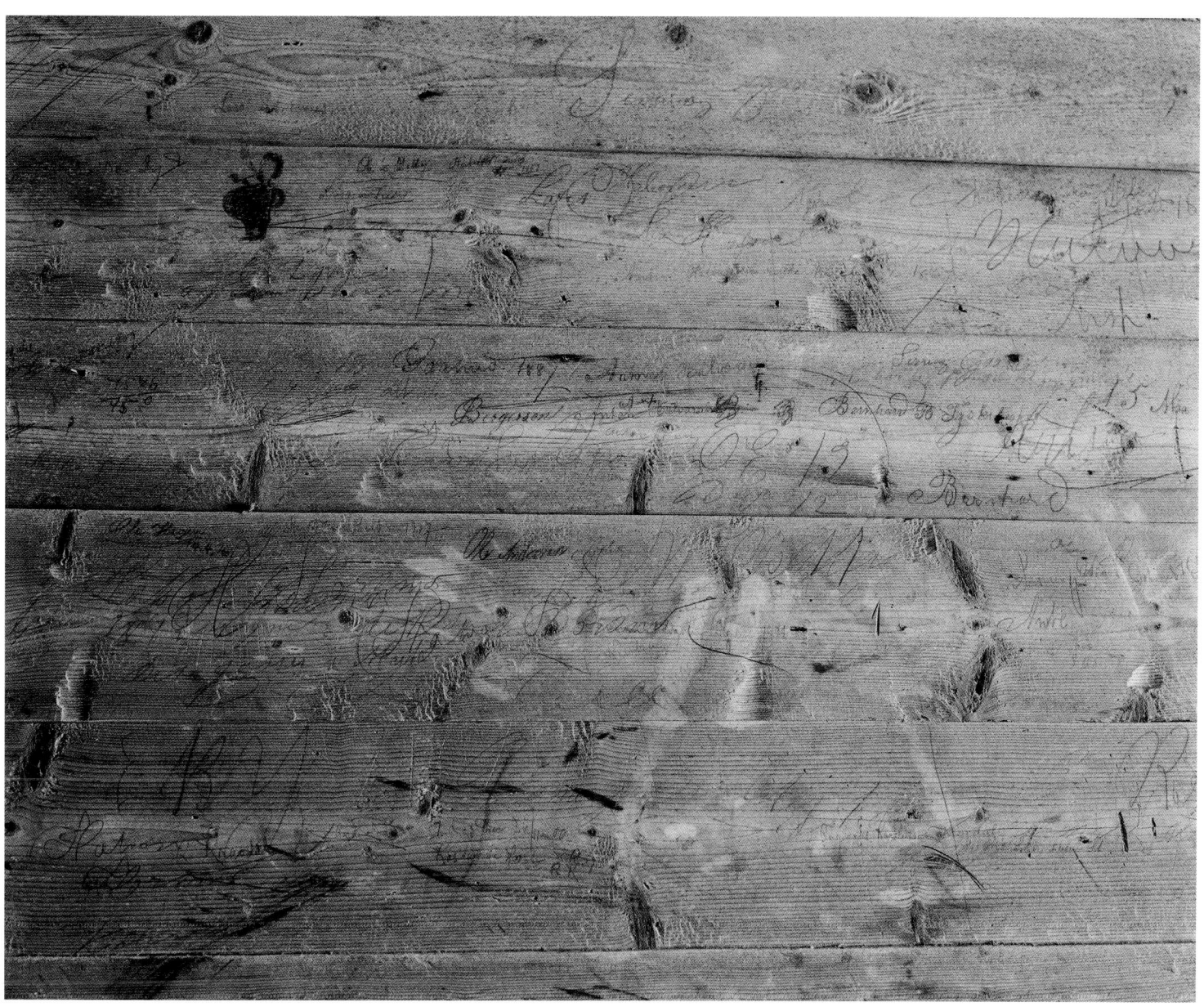

Ole Anderson's signature, Kjølen gård, 2008

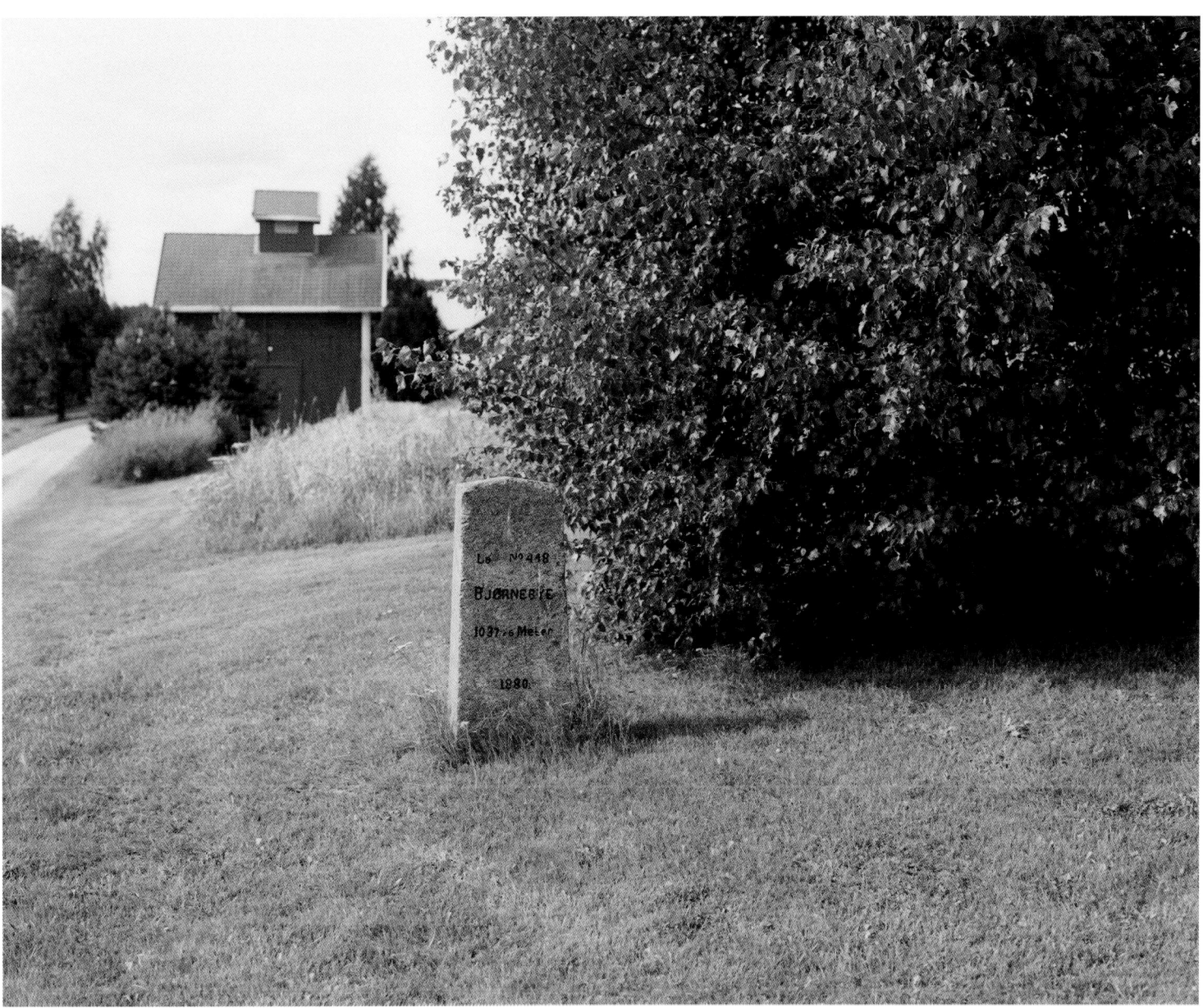

Bjørneby gård, 2008

Adolf Bjørneby
Kjølen in Åsnes
24th September 1880

Ole Anderson, from Strandrøningen farm, has worked for me for the last
four seasons. During this time, he behaved well and properly and was reliable.
He participated in all of the odd farm work, is strong, healthy, and very capable.
He has displayed a particular attention to and predisposition for all kinds
of handiwork, particularly carpentry. As he now intends to leave me, I will
not hesitate to recommend him to the best and wish him good luck on his
life's journey.

Adolf Bjørneby

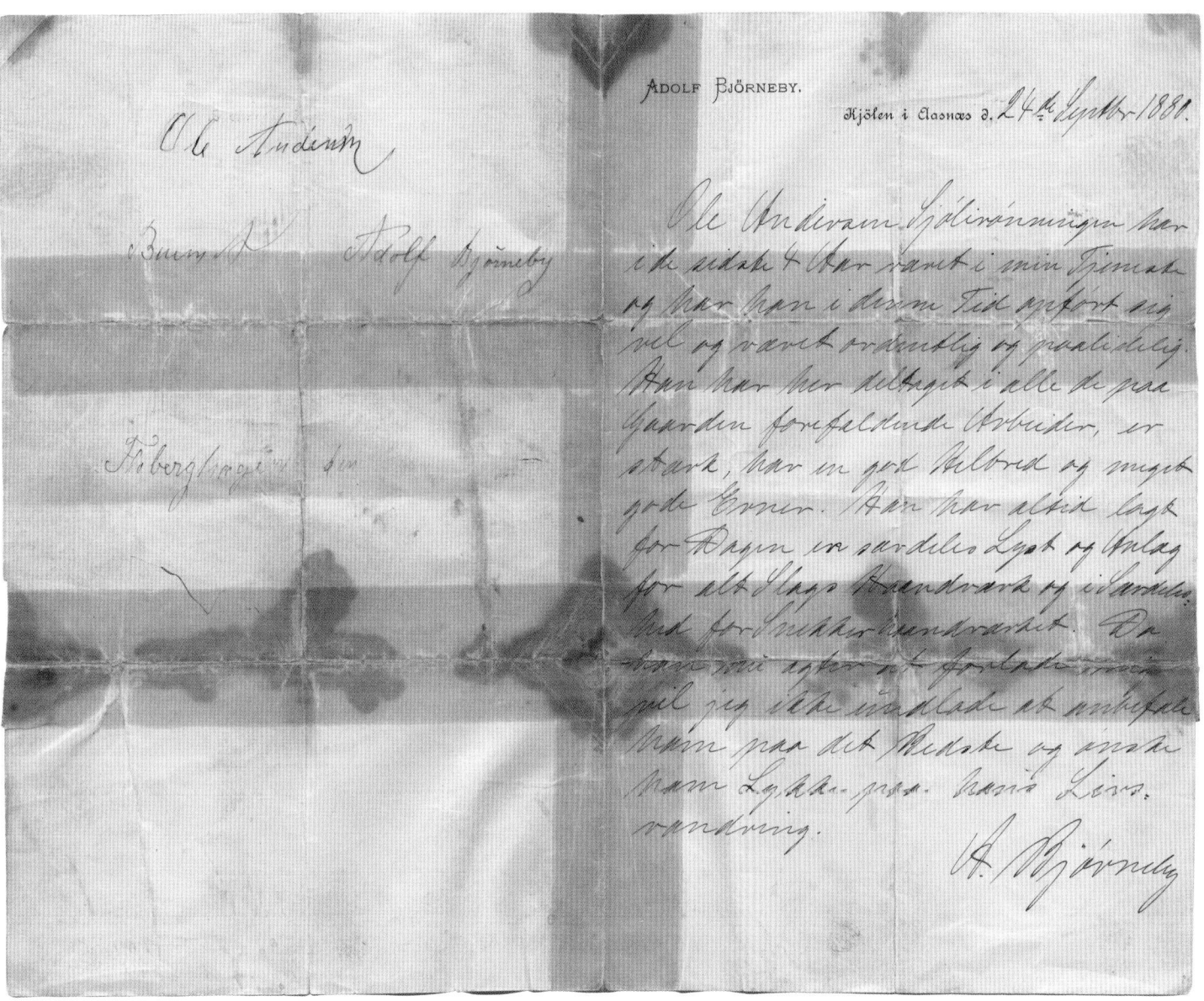

Letter of recommendation for Ole Anderson, 1880

Gamle Landet,
Old Country

Proving Up

From Tractor
to Camera

PROVING UP

Although I grew up on the farm, I was never directly involved in its operation. Instead, my chores were those typical for any kid: cleaning the house, mowing the lawn, and feeding our barn cats. After I learned to drive, I shuttled Mom and Dad between fields and brought them meals during harvest, but I never drove the tractors or the grain trucks. To this day I have still never learned how to drive a vehicle with a manual transmission.

I don't know if it was a conscious decision for my parents to exclude my siblings and me from the bulk of the farmwork. I do know that they had both grown up working on farms from a young age. Perhaps they wanted something different for us.

Whatever their reasons, there was one summer when Dad changed his mind. When I was around ten years old, he wanted to teach the three of us a lesson about how easy we had it. He forced us out of bed at 6 a.m. to pick weeds. He dropped us off in the field with work gloves and lunches and retrieved us in the afternoons, noting our slow progress. We tried to make a game out of it, but there was nothing fun about walking up and down the quarter section pulling and tugging, tossing and sweating. Mom took pity on us a few times and joined our ranks to boost morale—or just to bring us home early. After a week, we weren't done weeding the beans. Dad gave up all hope of us conquering the rest of his crops and gave us each fifty dollars instead.

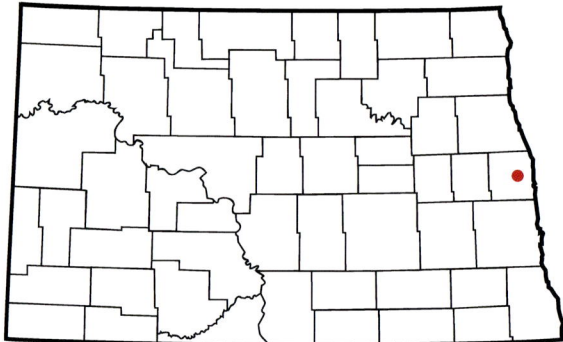

Map of North Dakota,
● Christianson Farm

Mom was never going to marry a farmer, much less be one, even though she had been "well trained for it." However, her fate was sealed when she met my father on a blind date. She would always help him out in the field, even when she was working as a nurse in town. Then when Grandpa Everett died, she became Dad's sole "hired hand"—his words, not mine.

Twelve hundred acres is just manageable for the two of them alone. They work symbiotically. While Dad plants in the spring, Mom prepares the next field by cultivating it. While Dad combines in the fall, Mom hauls the crops. She either takes them home to be stored in grain bins or brings them to local elevators in Buxton, Shelly, or Alton to fulfill contracts. Contracts are the safest way for my parents to hedge their bets: they lock in a price before the crop is even planted and are guaranteed that money when crops are delivered at harvest. Over the winter, they sell everything that is stored at home—when the prices are right—and haul it to the elevator. From there, the crops can go anywhere. One year, our soybeans were part of a shipment to Norway, where they were dumped in the fjords to feed the fish.

In general, now is a good time to be a farmer: the demand for ethanol has set record prices for corn, which has likewise spiked the prices for all edible crops to maintain a balance among the world's commodities. My parents never let themselves get carried away and instead get by with what they have. They use older machinery and fund their operation through cash reserves they have built up over time. Their livelihood is at the mercy of Mother Nature and global markets, and they try their best to prepare for all the *what if*s.

However, they are still evasive about the biggest question: what will happen to the Christianson farm in the end? My parents should have many years ahead of them to run it. Even though Dad will be turning 60 this year, neither his father, nor his grandpa, nor his great-grandfather ever really retired in the conventional sense. To deflect speculation about the future, Dad is always quick to say, only half jokingly, "Girls can be farmers, too, you know."

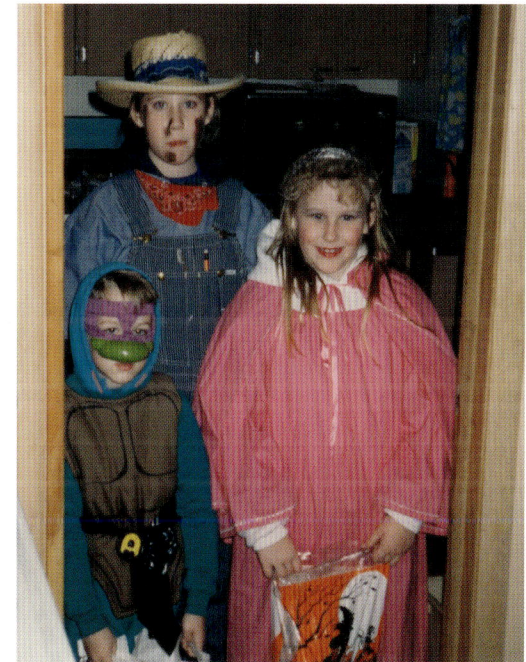

Sarah as farmer for Halloween, 1992

26

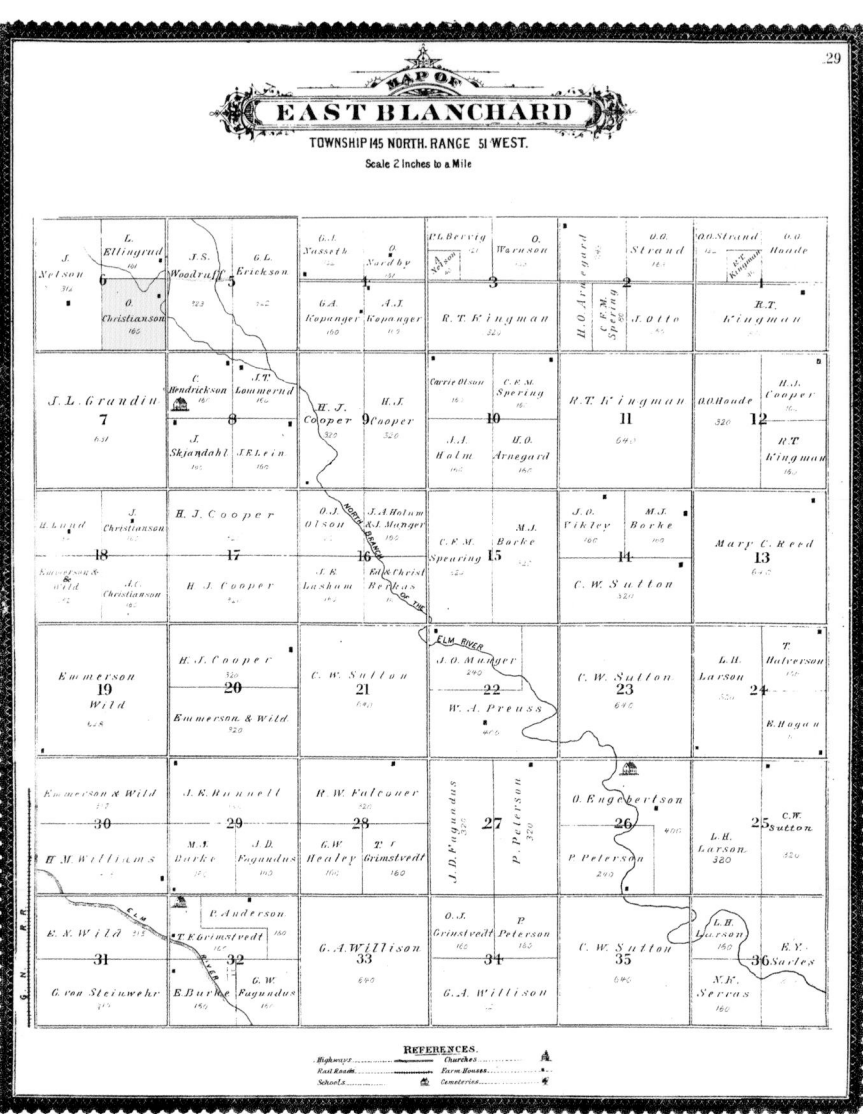

East Blanchard (Bloomfield) Township map, 1892

THE UNITED STATES OF AMERICA,

To all to whom these presents shall come, Greeting:

(4—405.)

Homestead Certificate No. *1596*

APPLICATION *6870*

Whereas There has been deposited in the GENERAL LAND OFFICE of the United States a CERTIFICATE OF THE REGISTER of the LAND OFFICE at *Fargo Dakota Territory* , whereby it appears that, pursuant to the Act of Congress approved 20th May, 1862, "To secure Homesteads to Actual Settlers on the Public Domain," and the acts supplemental thereto, the claim of *Olai Christianson* has been established and duly consummated, in conformity to law, for the *south-east quarter of section six in township one hundred and forty-five north of range fifty-one west of the Fifth Principal Meridian in Dakota Territory containing one hundred and sixty acres*

according to the OFFICIAL PLAT of the Survey of the said Land, returned to the GENERAL LAND OFFICE by the SURVEYOR GENERAL:

Now know ye, That there is, therefore, granted by the United States unto the said *Olai Christianson* the tract of Land above described: To have and to hold the said tract of Land, with the appurtenances thereof, unto the said *Olai Christianson* and to *his* heirs and assigns forever; subject to any vested and accrued water rights for mining, agricultural, manufacturing, or other purposes, and rights to ditches and reservoirs used in connection with such water rights, as may be recognized and acknowledged by the local customs, laws, and decisions of courts, and also subject to the right of the proprietor of a vein or lode to extract and remove his ore therefrom, should the same be found to penetrate or intersect the premises hereby granted, as provided by law.

In testimony whereof I, *Chester A. Arthur* , President of the United States of America, have caused these letters to be made Patent, and the seal of the GENERAL LAND OFFICE to be hereunto affixed.

Given under my hand, at the CITY OF WASHINGTON, the *fourth* day of *October* , in the year of our Lord one thousand eight hundred and *eighty-four* , and of the Independence of the United States the one hundred and *ninth* .

By the President: *Chester A Arthur*

By *M. McKean* , Secretary.

S W Clark , Recorder of the General Land Office.

RECORDED, Vol. *4* Page *340*

[12907—7,000.]

Homestead certificate, 1884

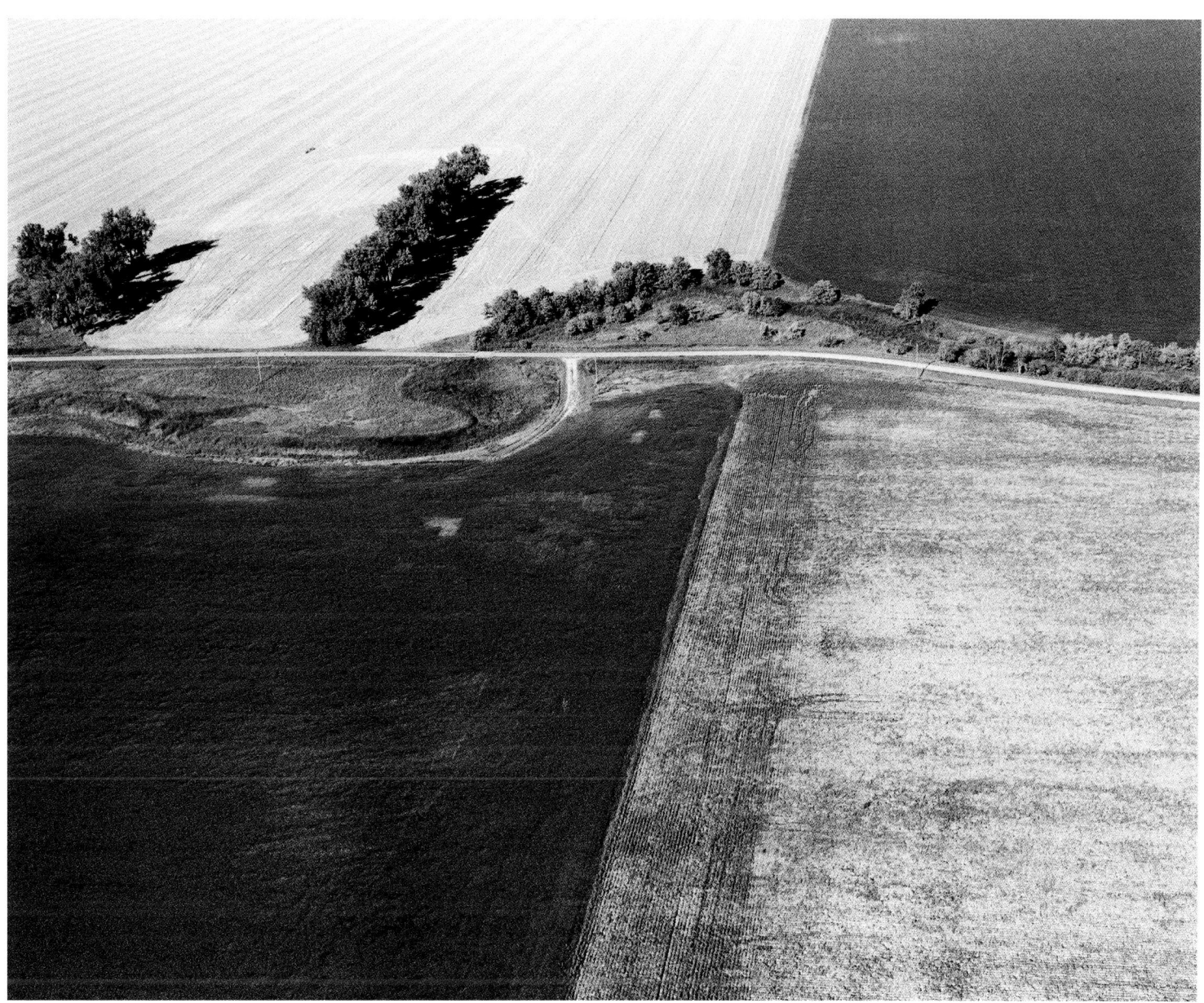

Christianson homestead with traces of buildings, 2007

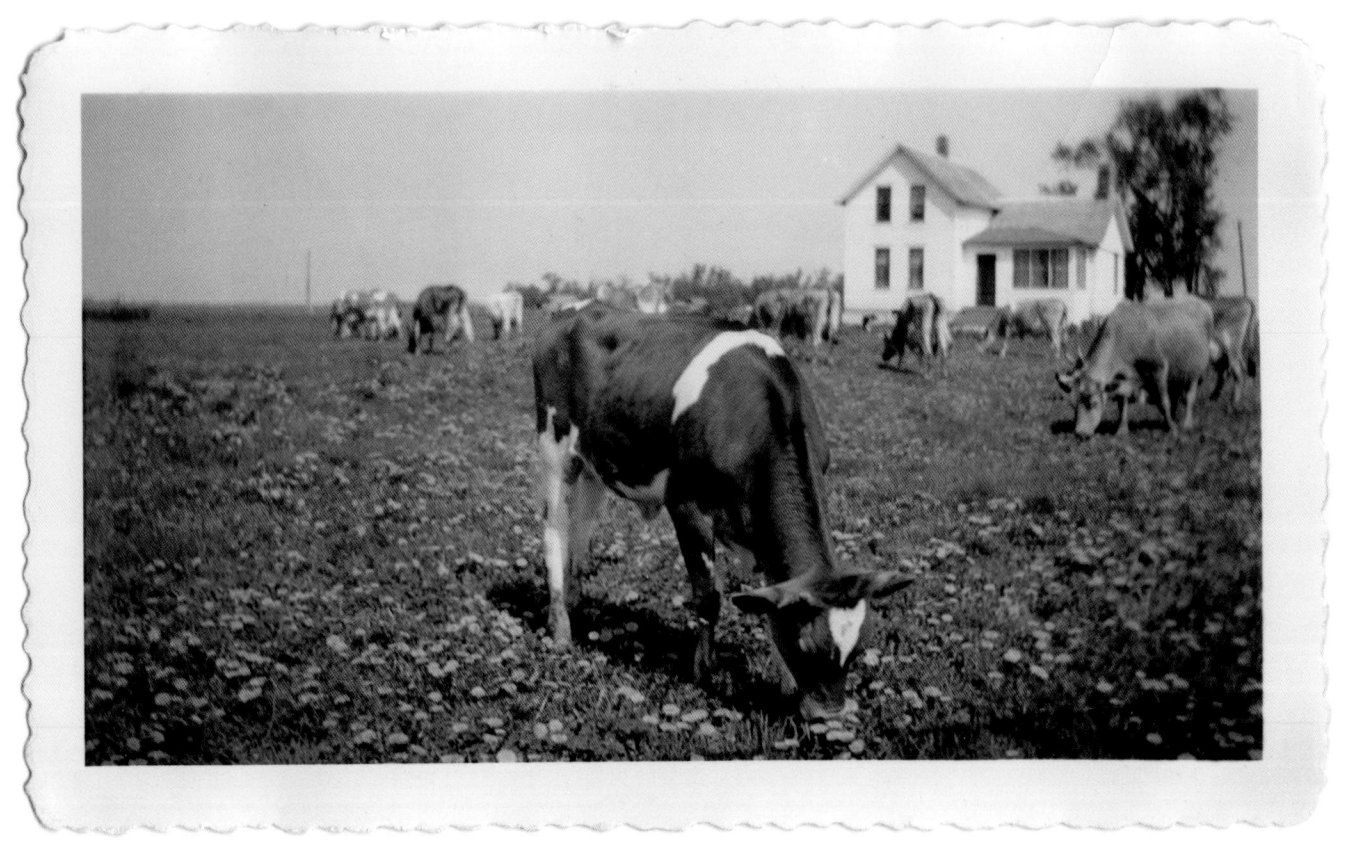

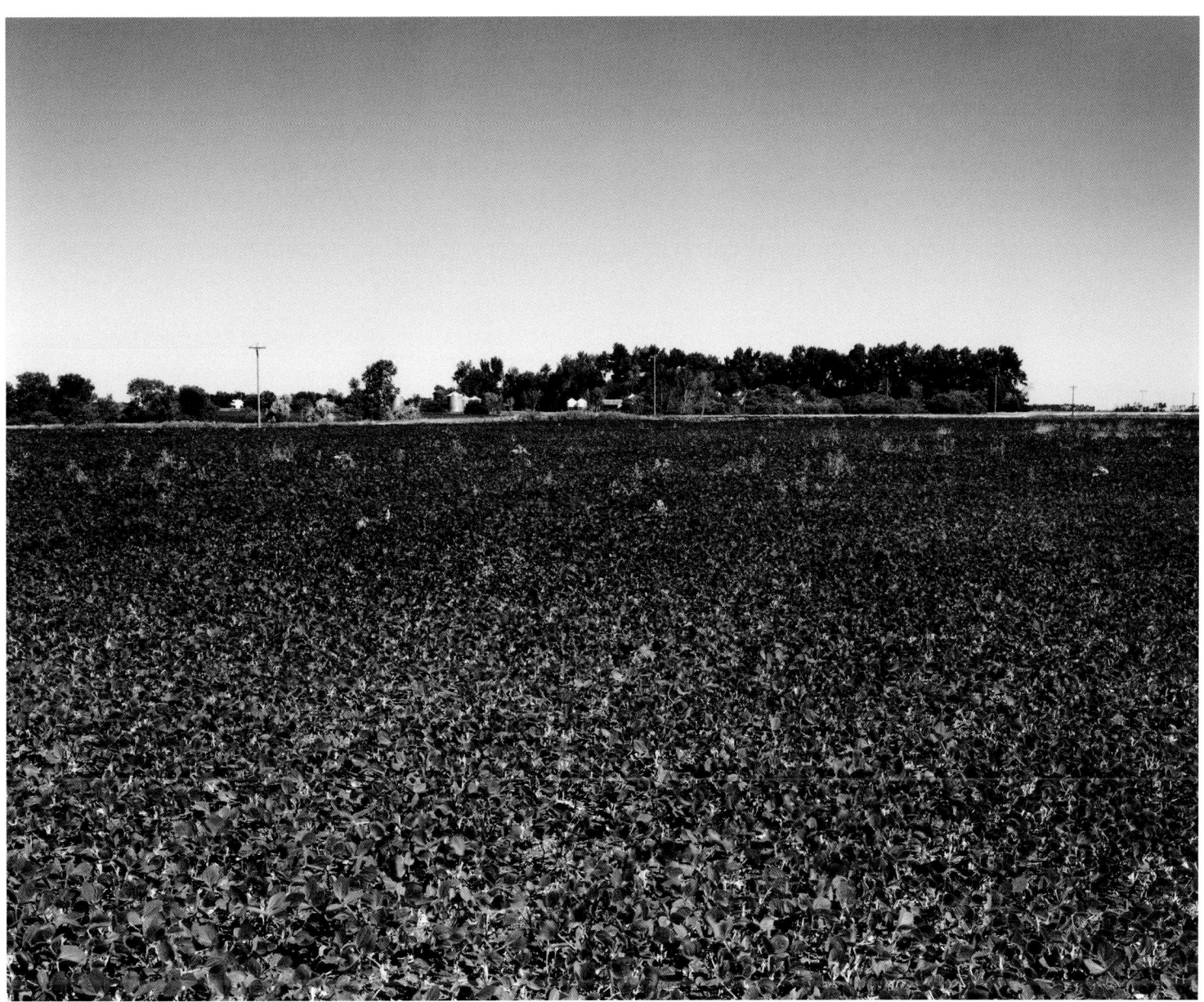

From homestead to field: 1942 (opposite) and 2007

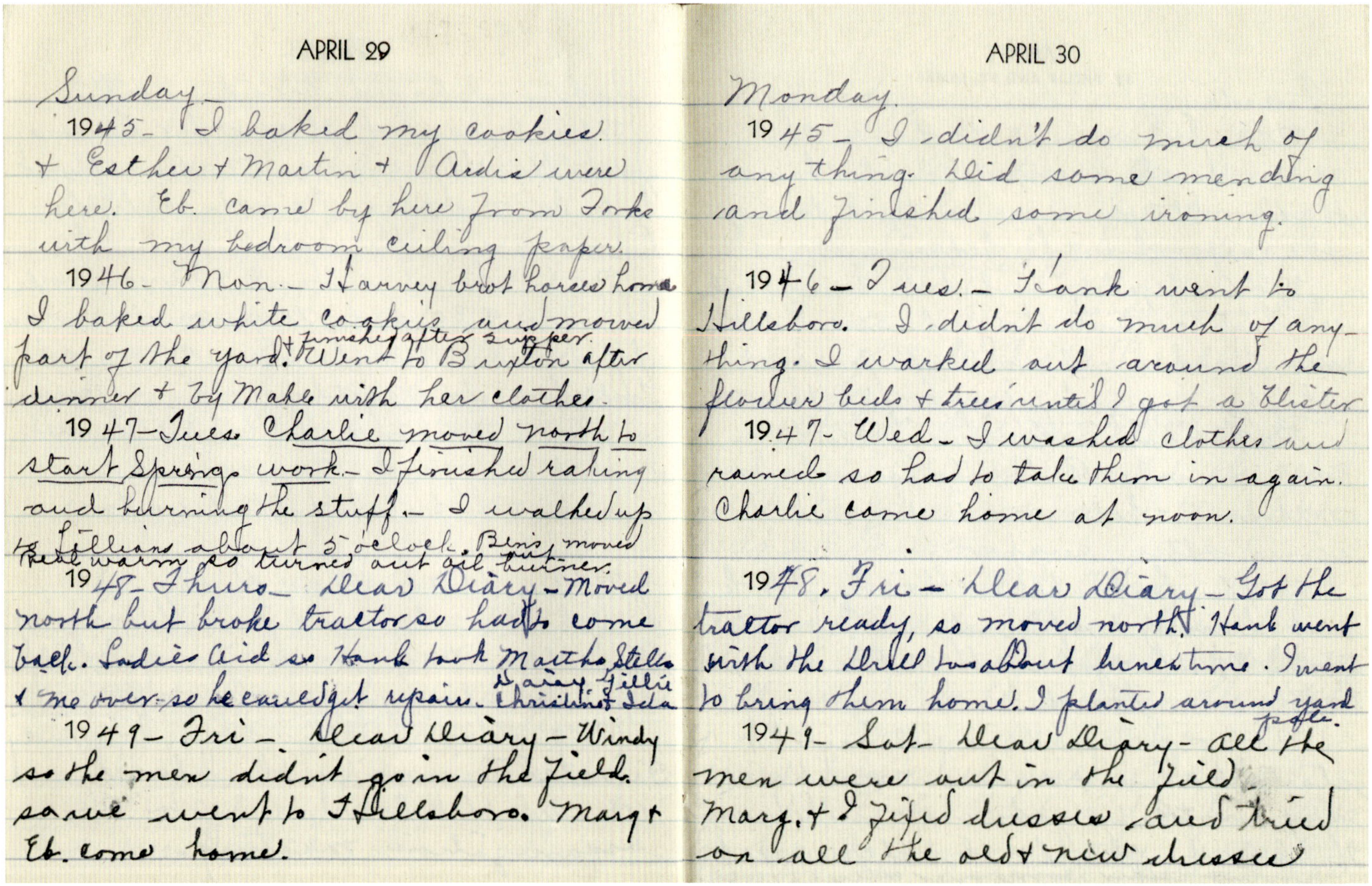

APRIL 29

Sunday.

1945 – I baked my cookies.
& Esther & Martin & Ardis were
here. Eb. came by here from Forks
with my bedroom ceiling paper.

1946 – Mon. – Harvey brot horses home
I baked white cookies and moved
part of the yard. Went to Buxton after
dinner & by Mabs with her clothes. *finished after supper.

1947 – Tues. Charlie moved north to
start Spring work. – I finished raking
and burning the stuff. – I walked up
to Lillians about 5 o'clock. Bens moved
Real warm so turned out oil burner.

1948 – Thurs. – Dear Diary – Moved
north but broke tractor so had to come
back. Ladies Aid so Hank took Martha Stella
& me over – so he could get repair. Daisy, Tillie
Christine & Ida

1949 – Fri. – Dear Diary – Windy
so the men didn't go in the field.
so we went to Hillsboro. Mary &
Eb. come home.

APRIL 30

Monday.

1945 – I didn't do much of
any thing. Did some mending
and finished some ironing.

1946 – Tues. – Frank went to
Hillsboro. I didn't do much of any-
thing. I worked out around the
flower beds & trees until I got a blister

1947 – Wed. – I washed clothes and
rained so had to take them in again.
Charlie come home at noon.

1948. Fri – Dear Diary – Got the
tractor ready, so moved north. Hank went
with the Drill was about lunch time. I went
to bring them home. I planted around yard

1949 – Sat. – Dear Diary – All the men
men were out in the field
Mary & I fixed dresses and tried
on all the old & new dresses

Excerpt from Great-grandma Claire's diary about spring work, 1945–1949

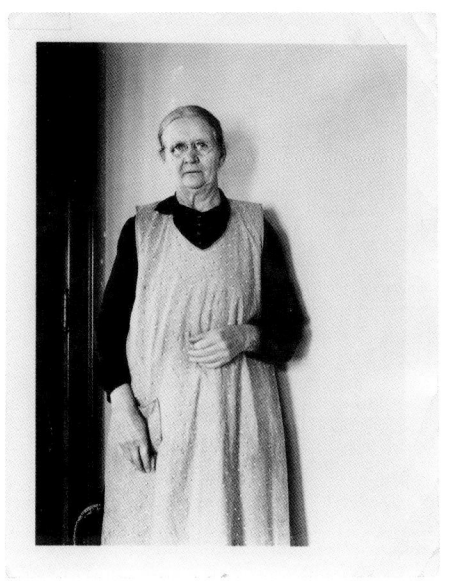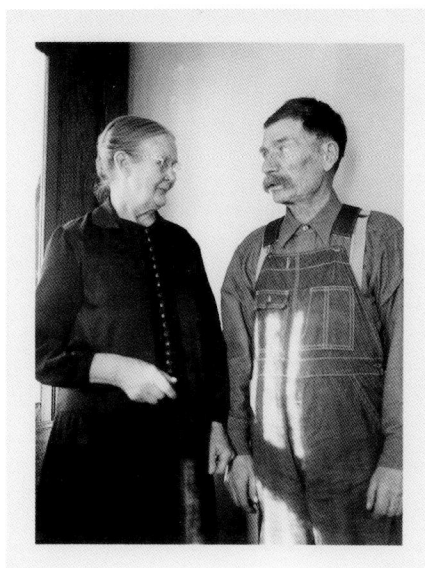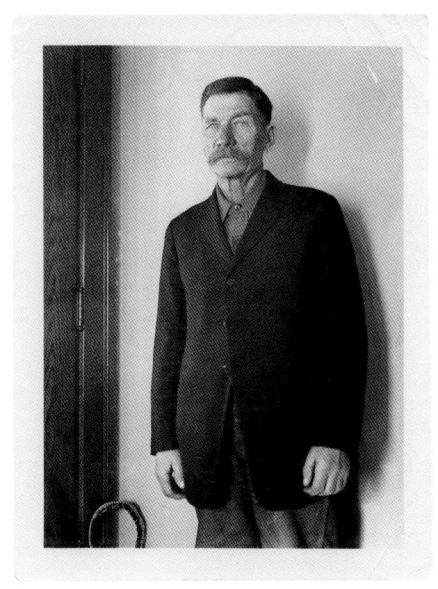

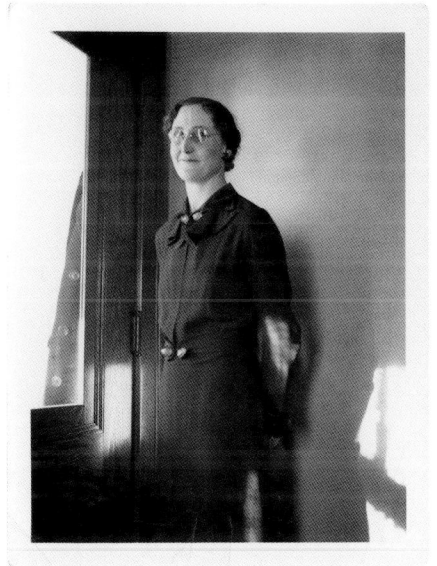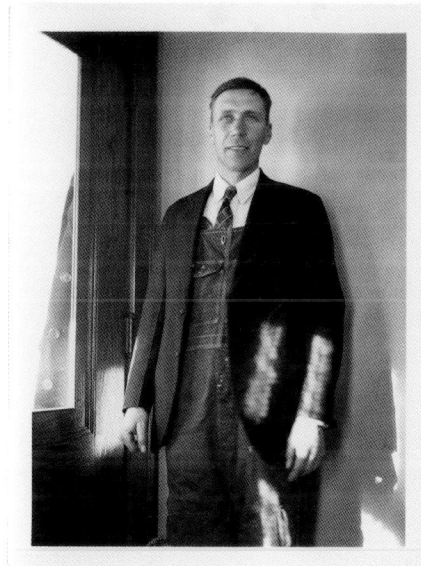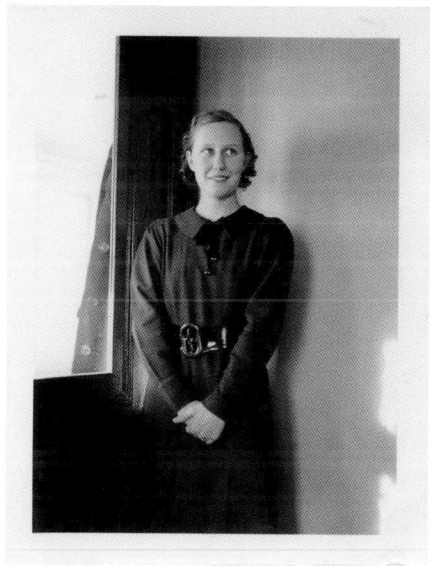

Grandma Margaret with her parents and grandparents, 1937

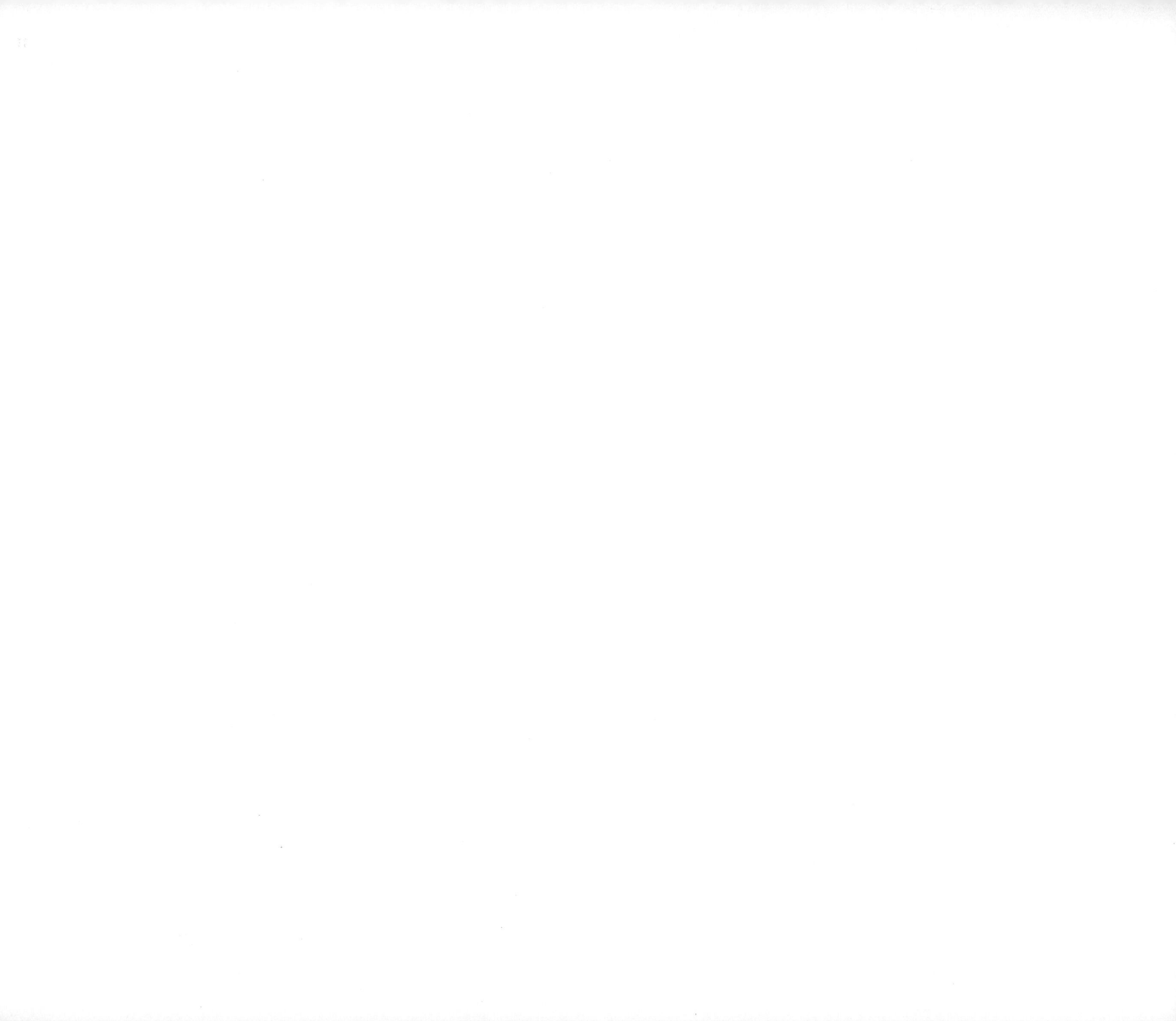

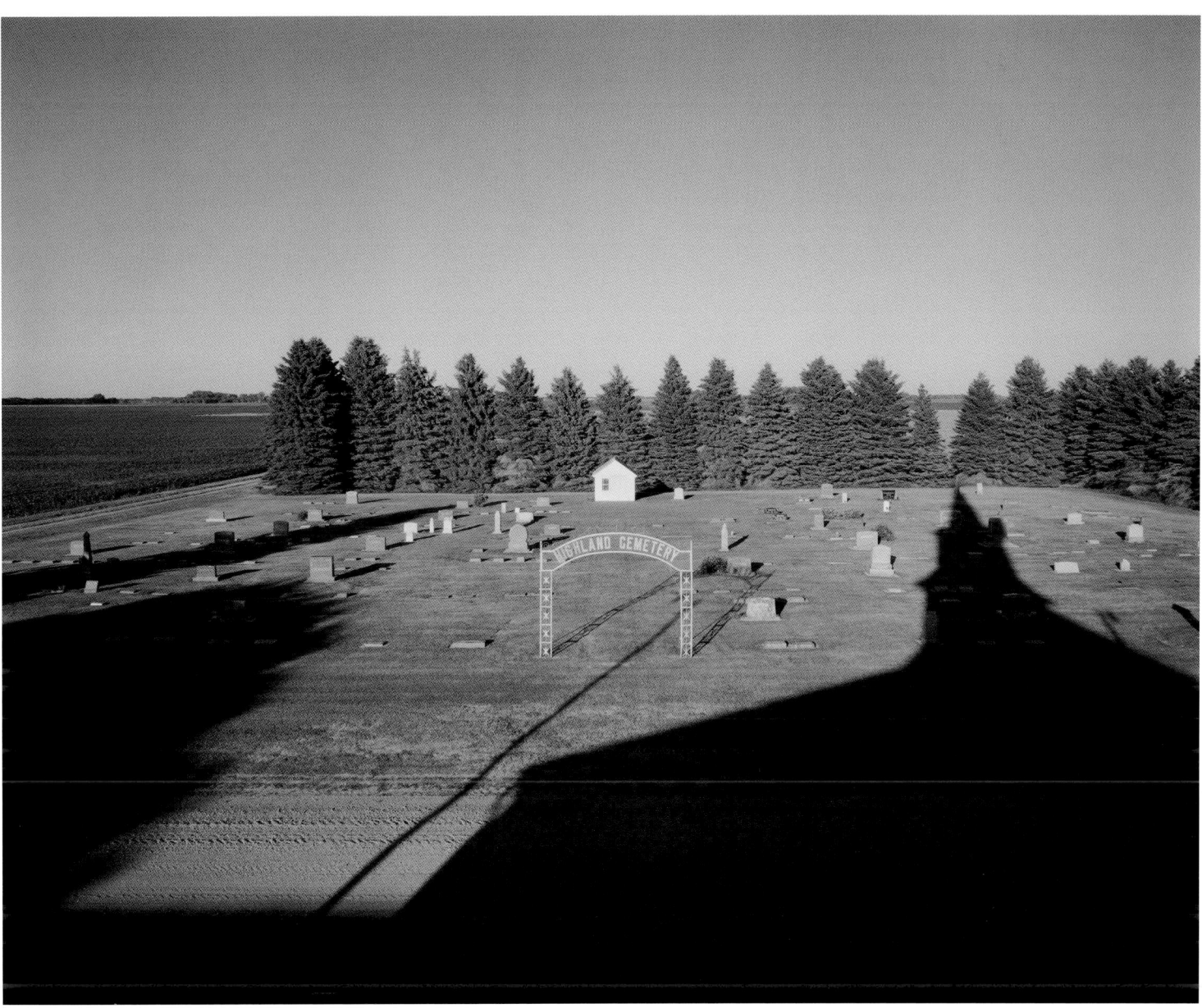

Highland Lutheran Church and Cemetery, 2007

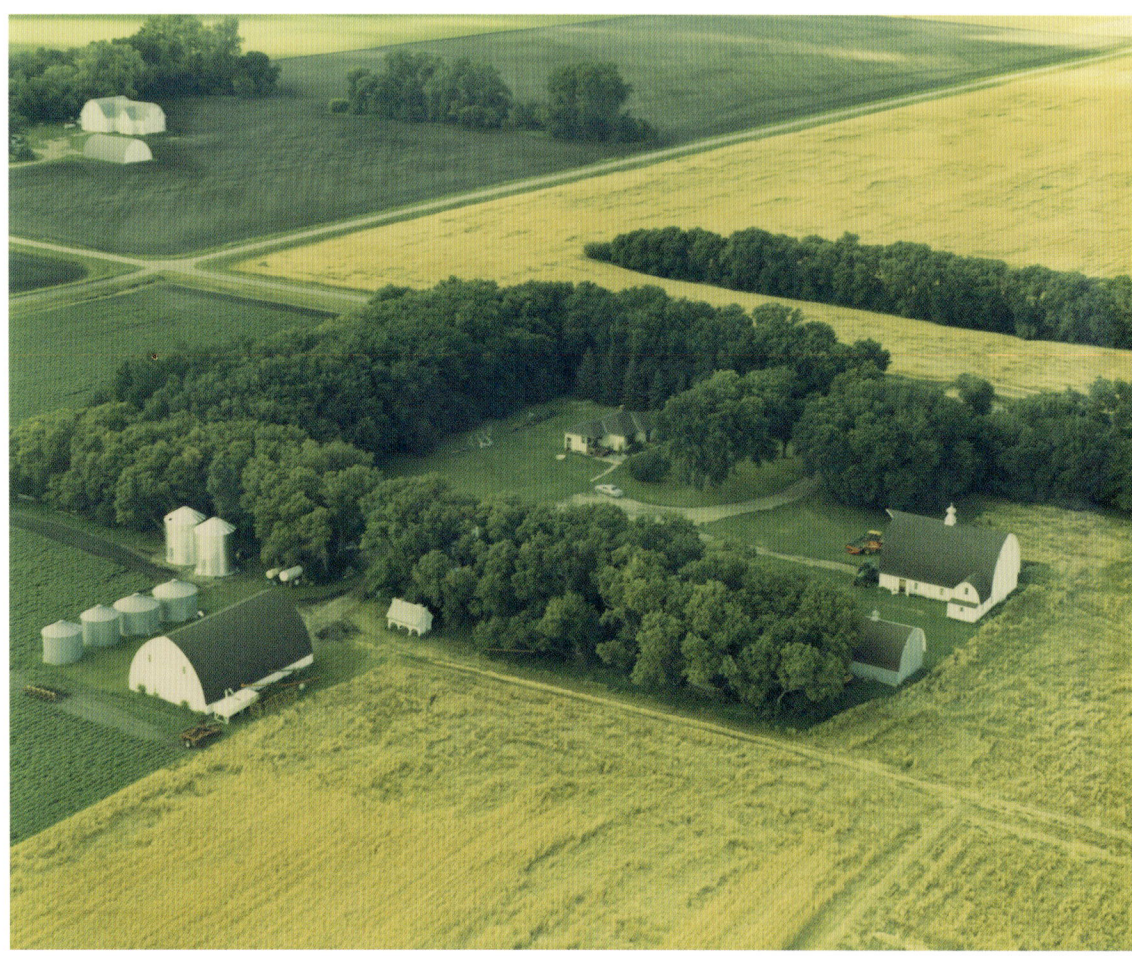

Christianson farm before Dutch elm disease, 1984

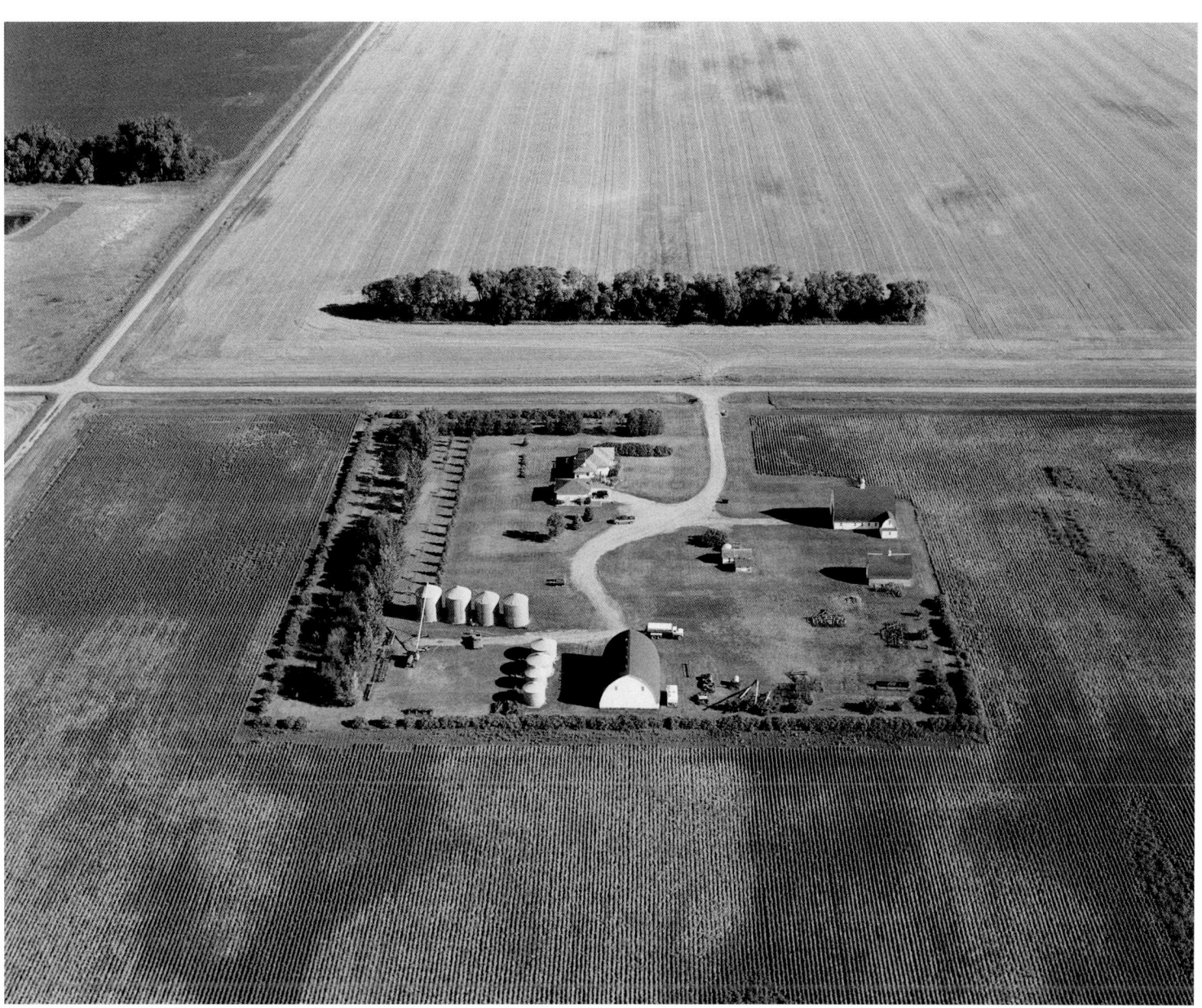

Christianson farm with new saplings, 2007

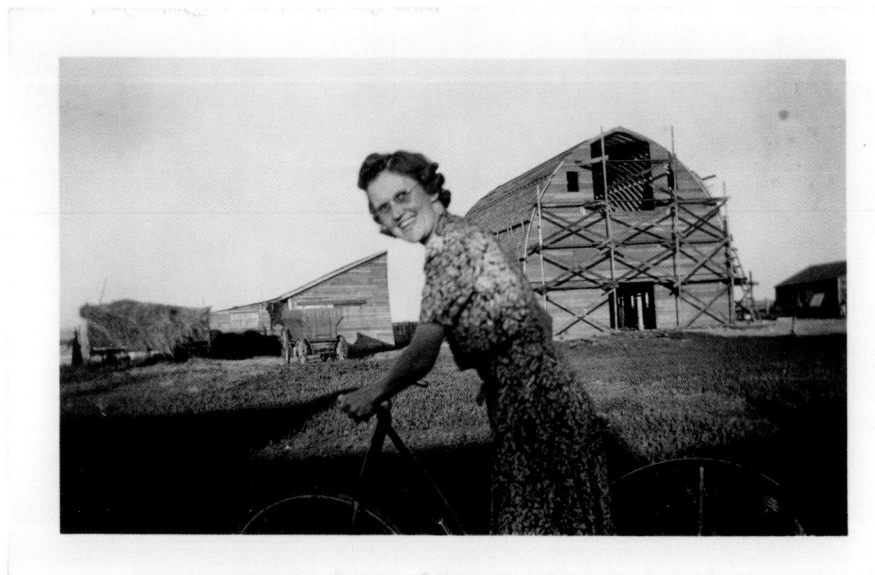

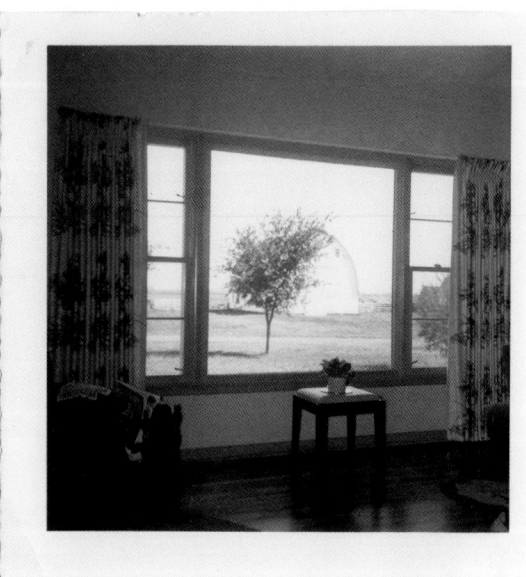

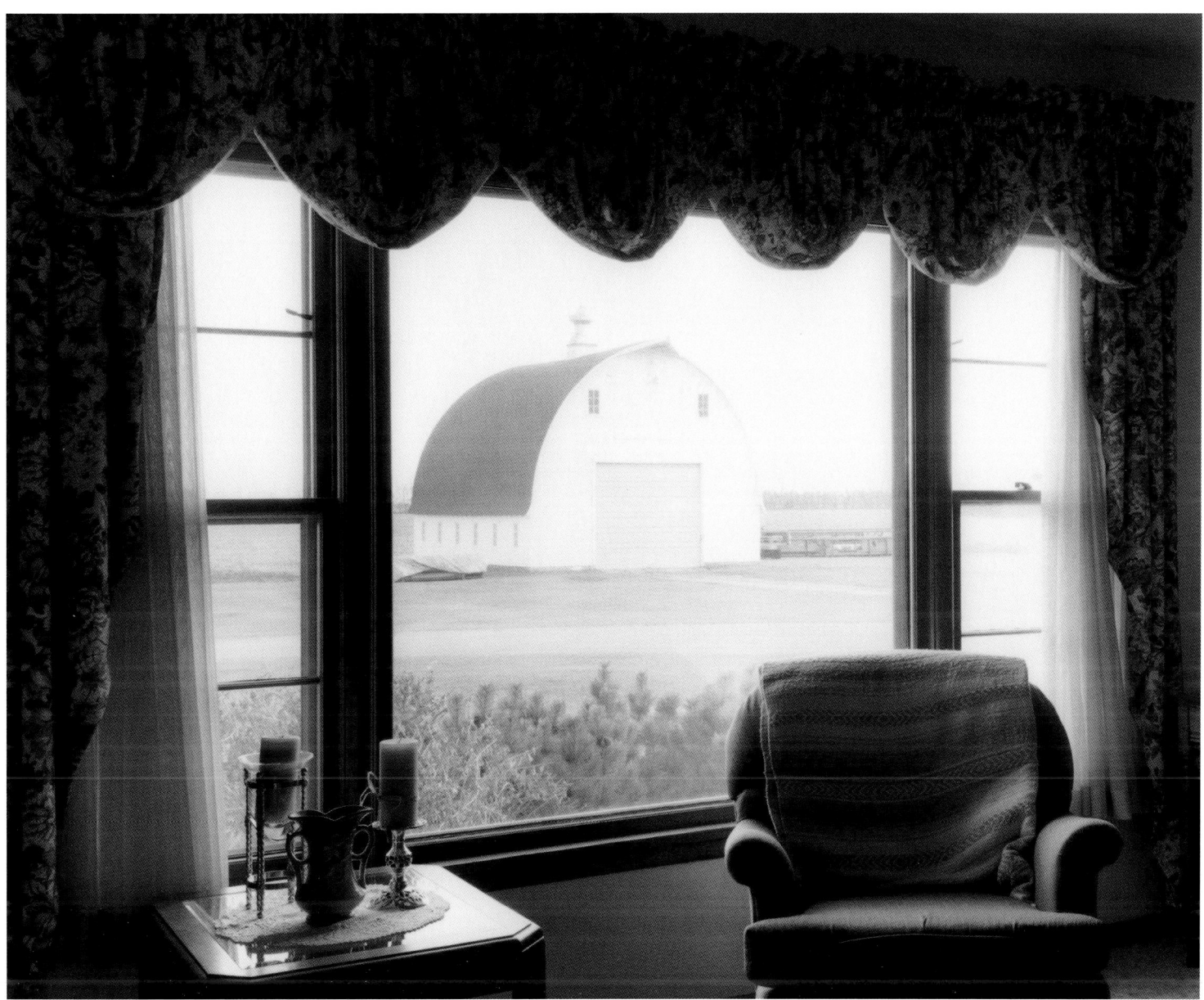

The barn: 1941 and 1953 (opposite), 2006

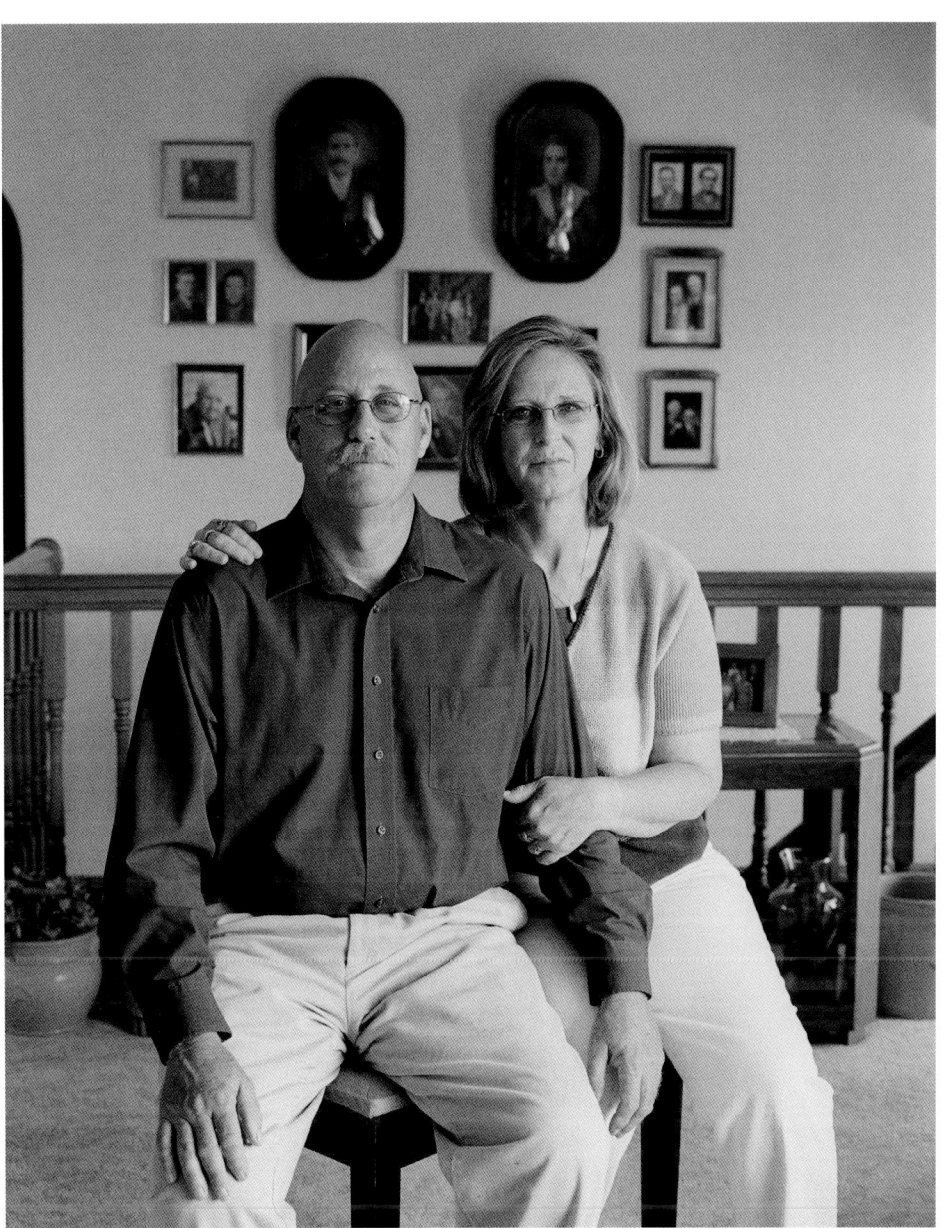

My parents, Dale and Rose Christianson, 2008

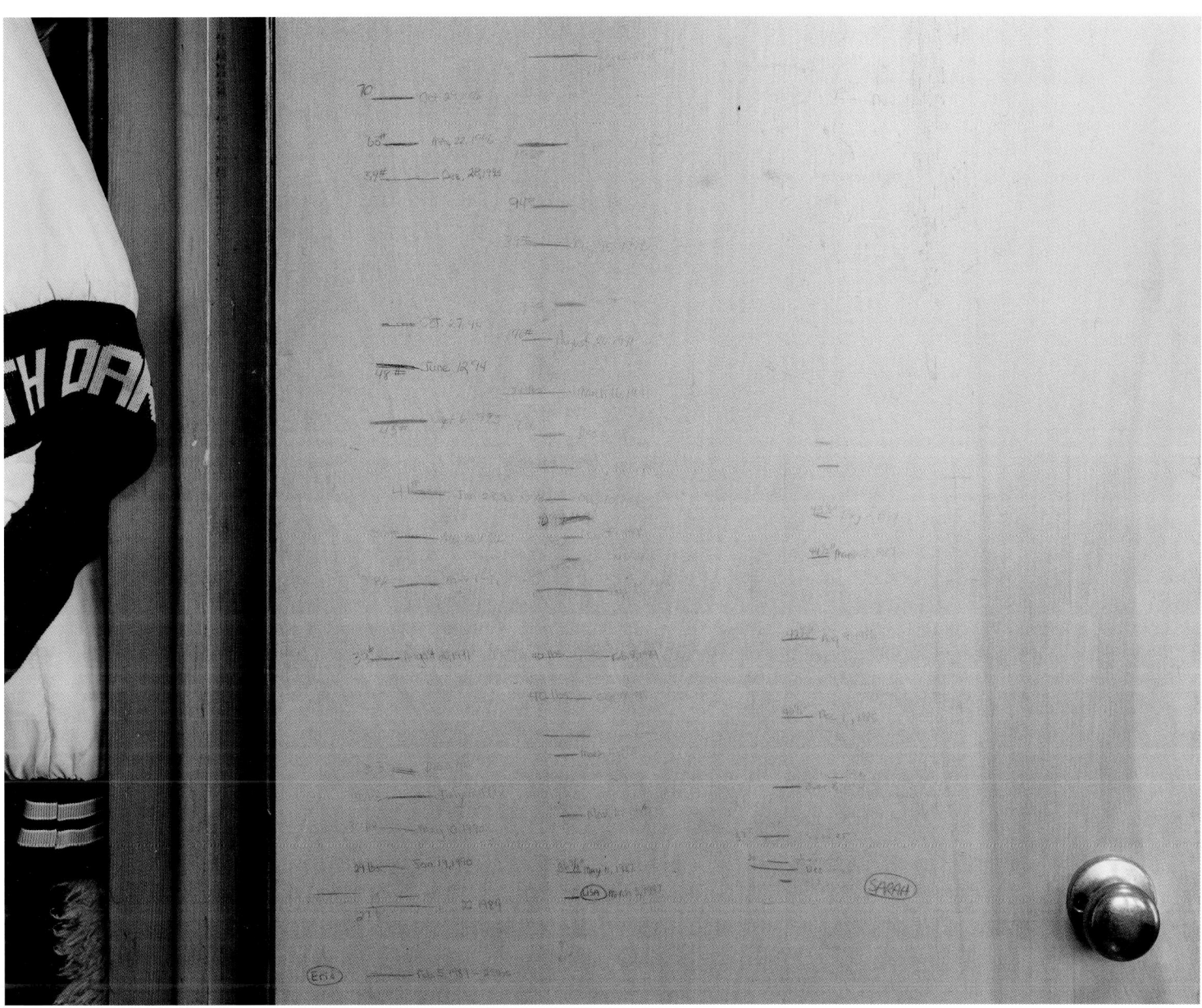

Closet door, 2008

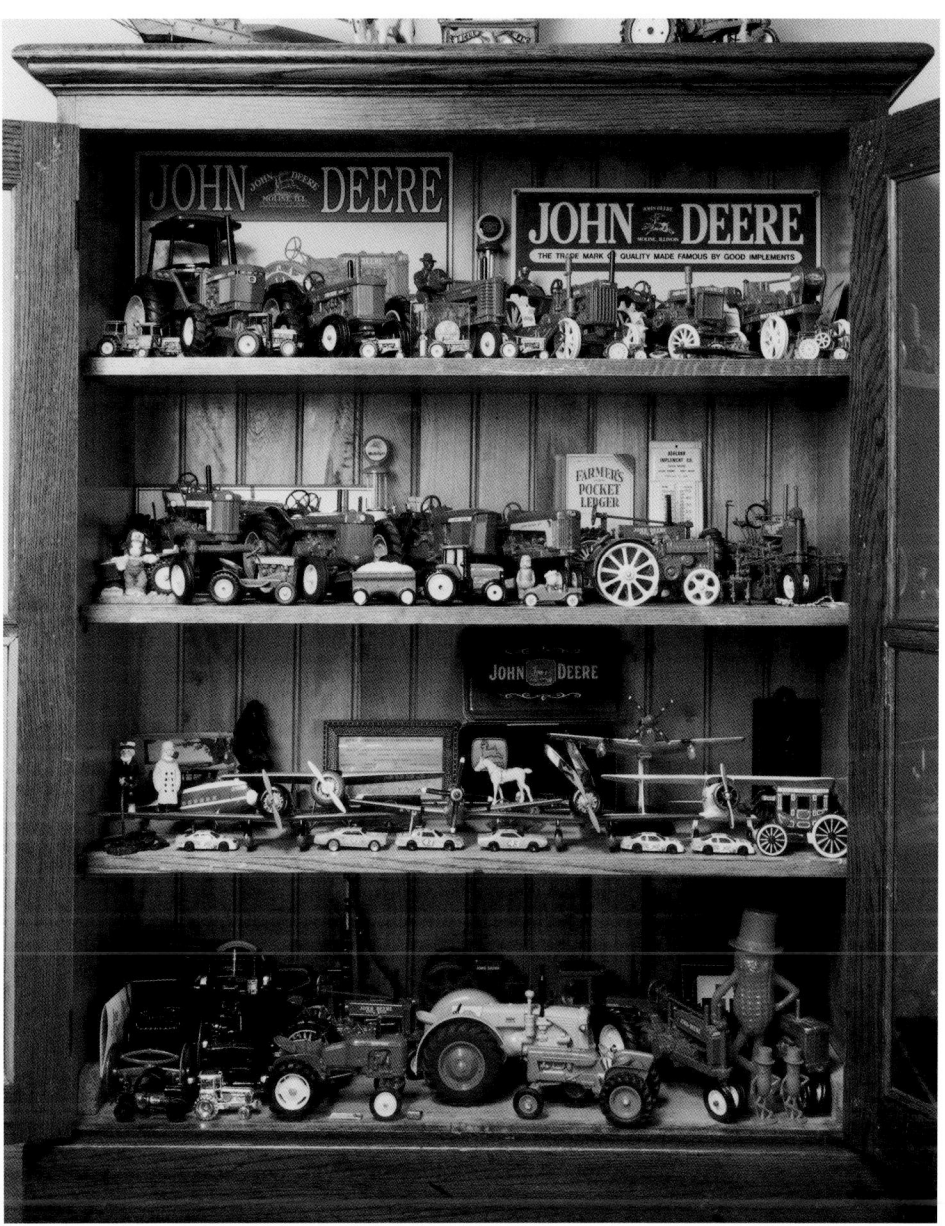

Dad's John Deere collection, 2008

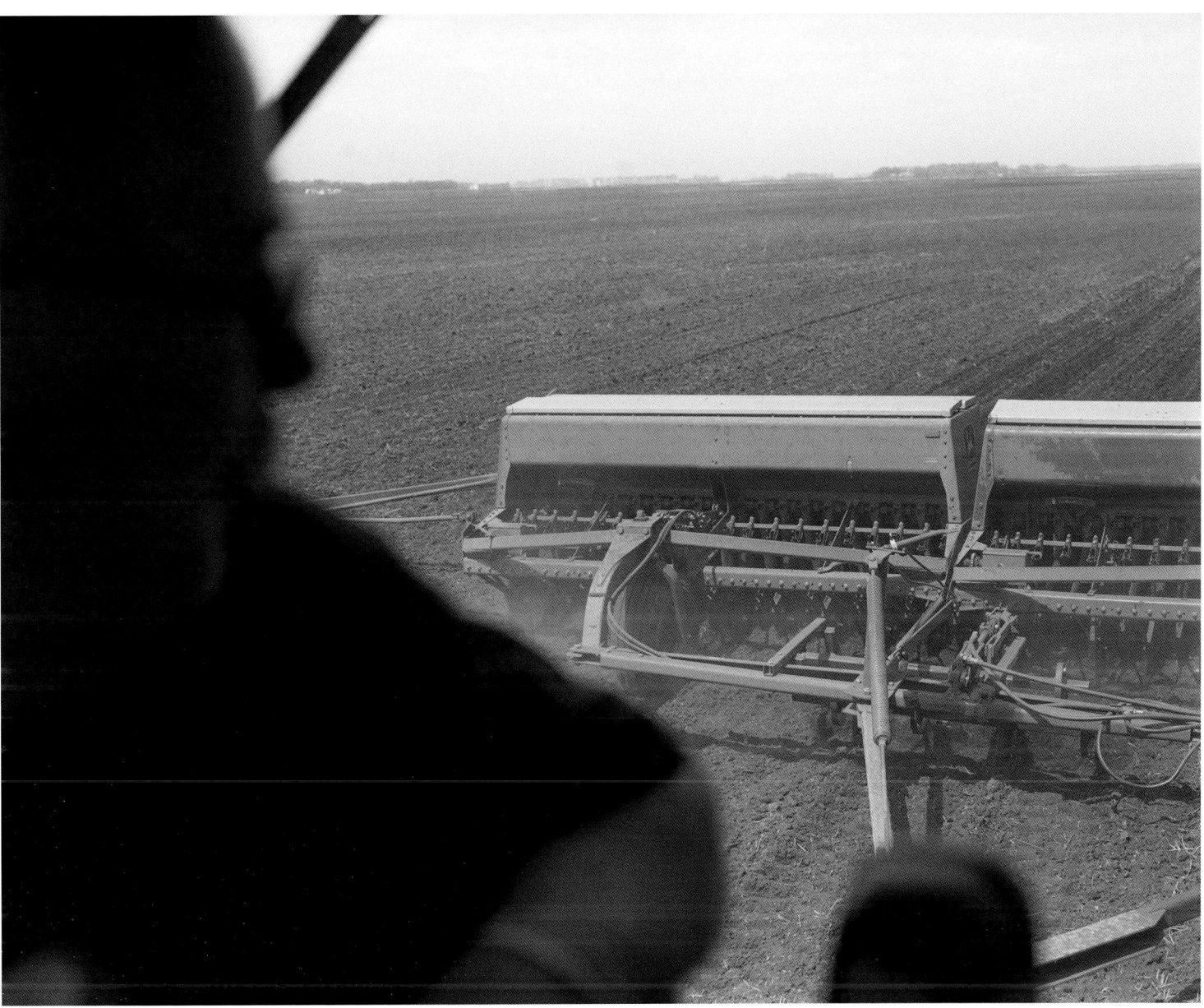

Dad, spring planting, 2007

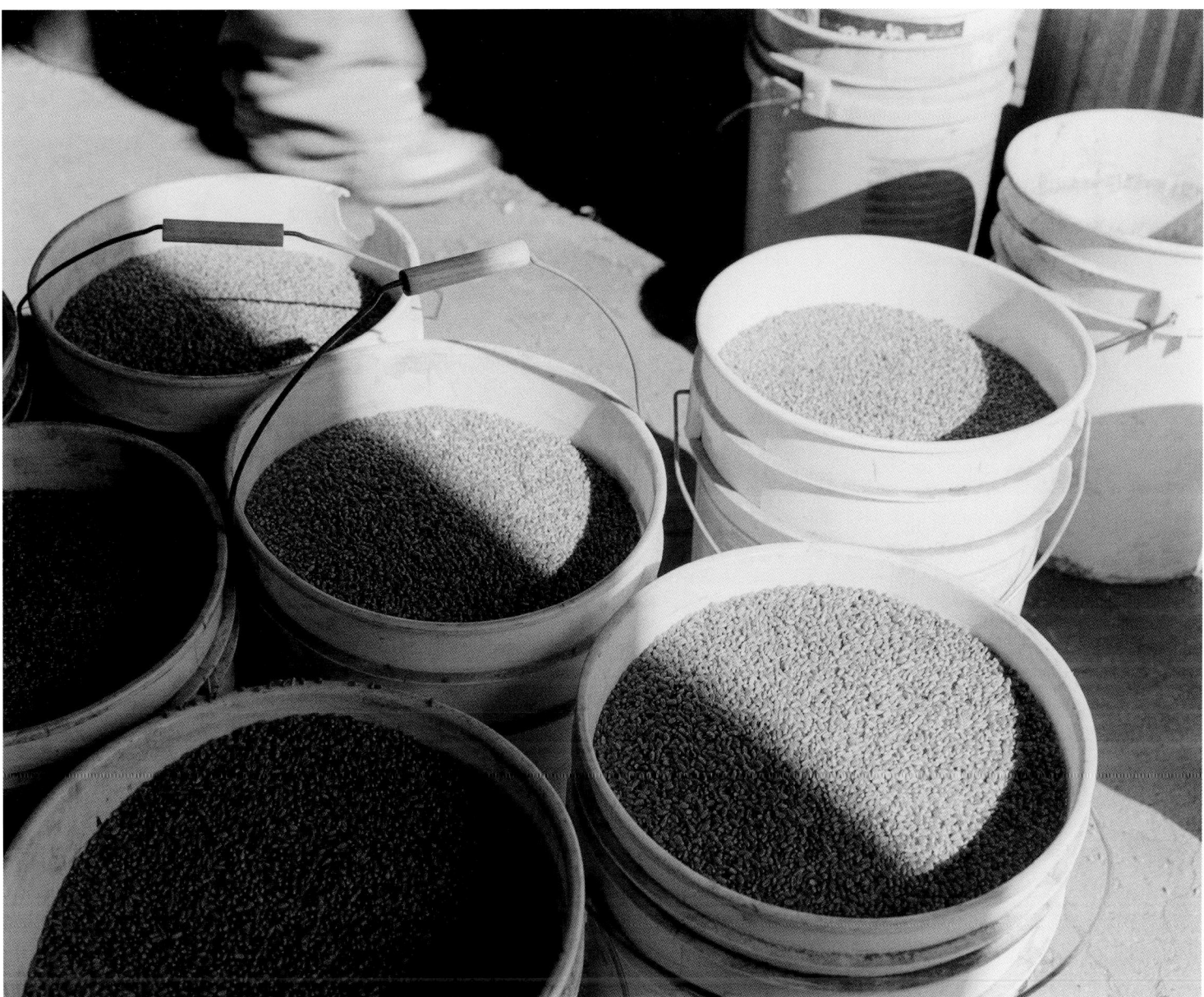

Wheat seed, 2007

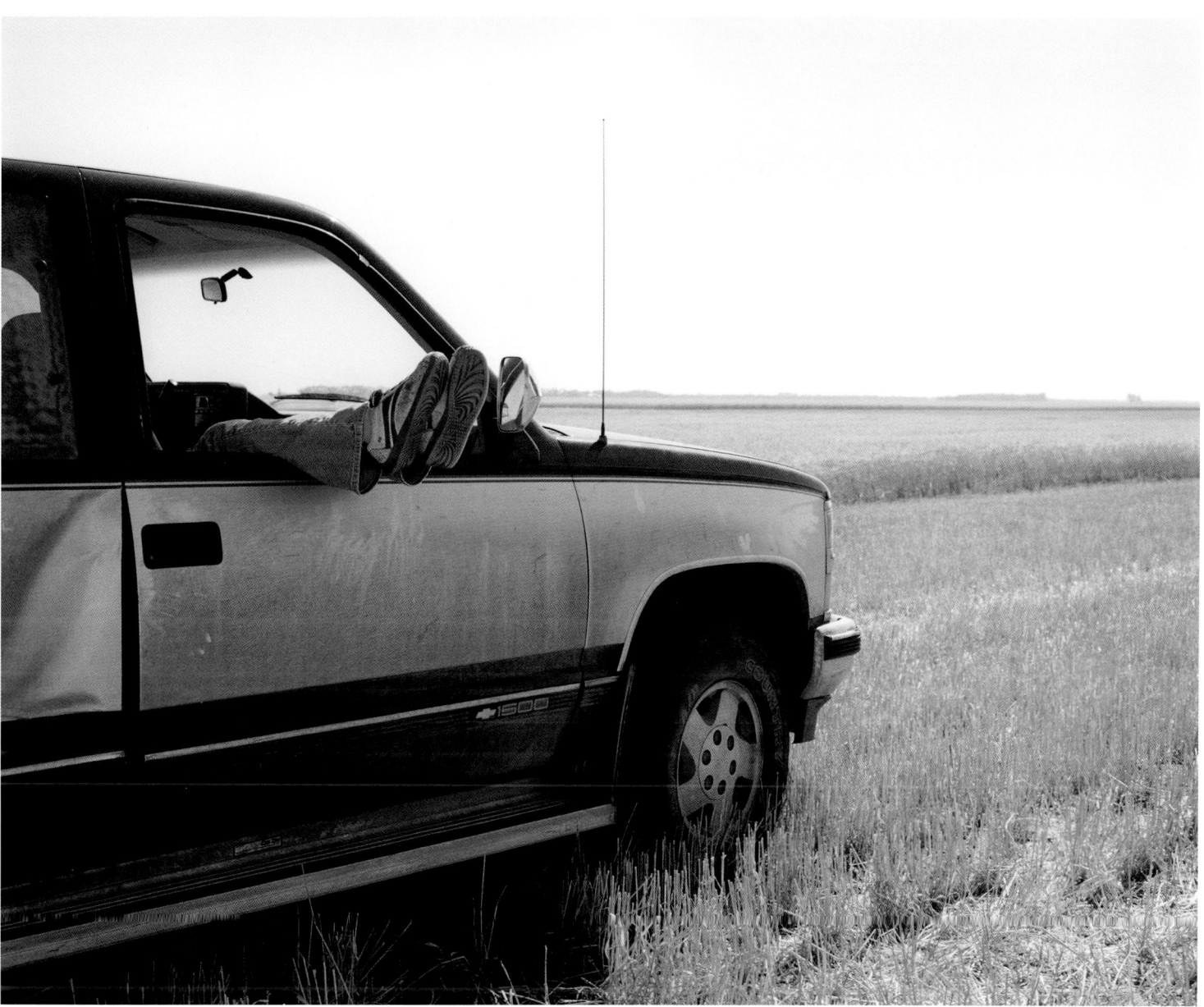

Mom, wheat harvest, 2007

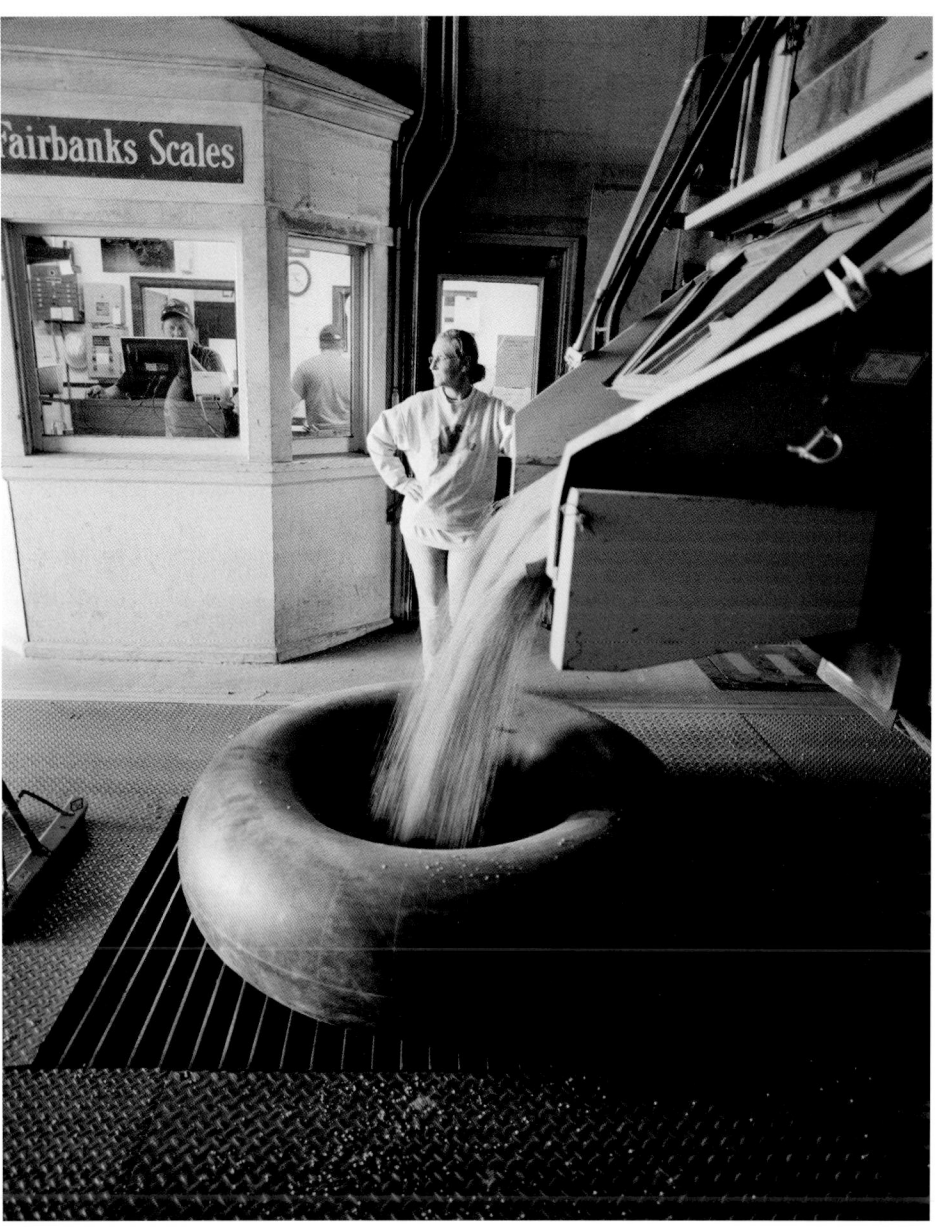

Mom unloading soybeans, Shelly Elevator, 2008

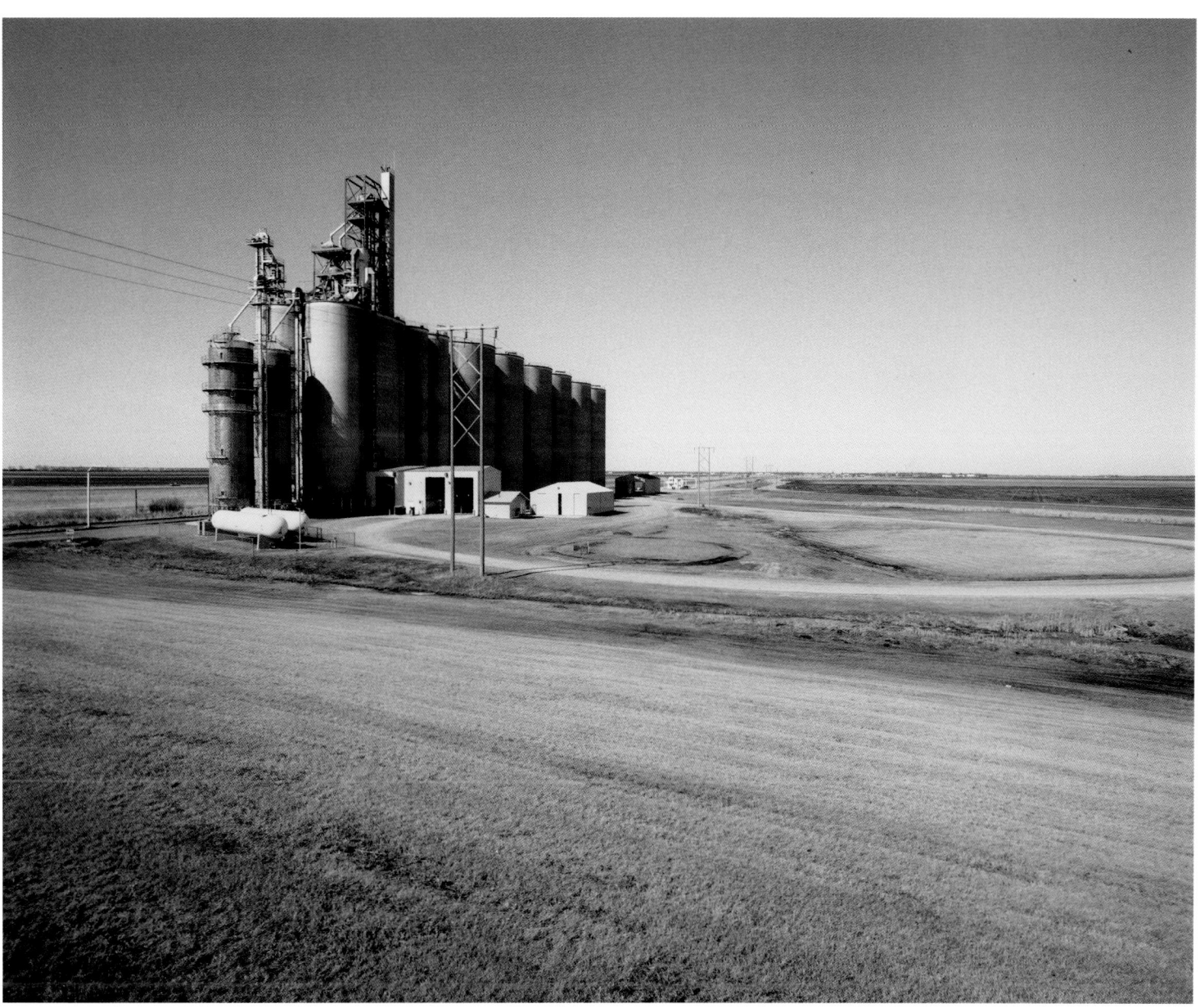

Alton Grain Terminal, near Hillsboro, 2012

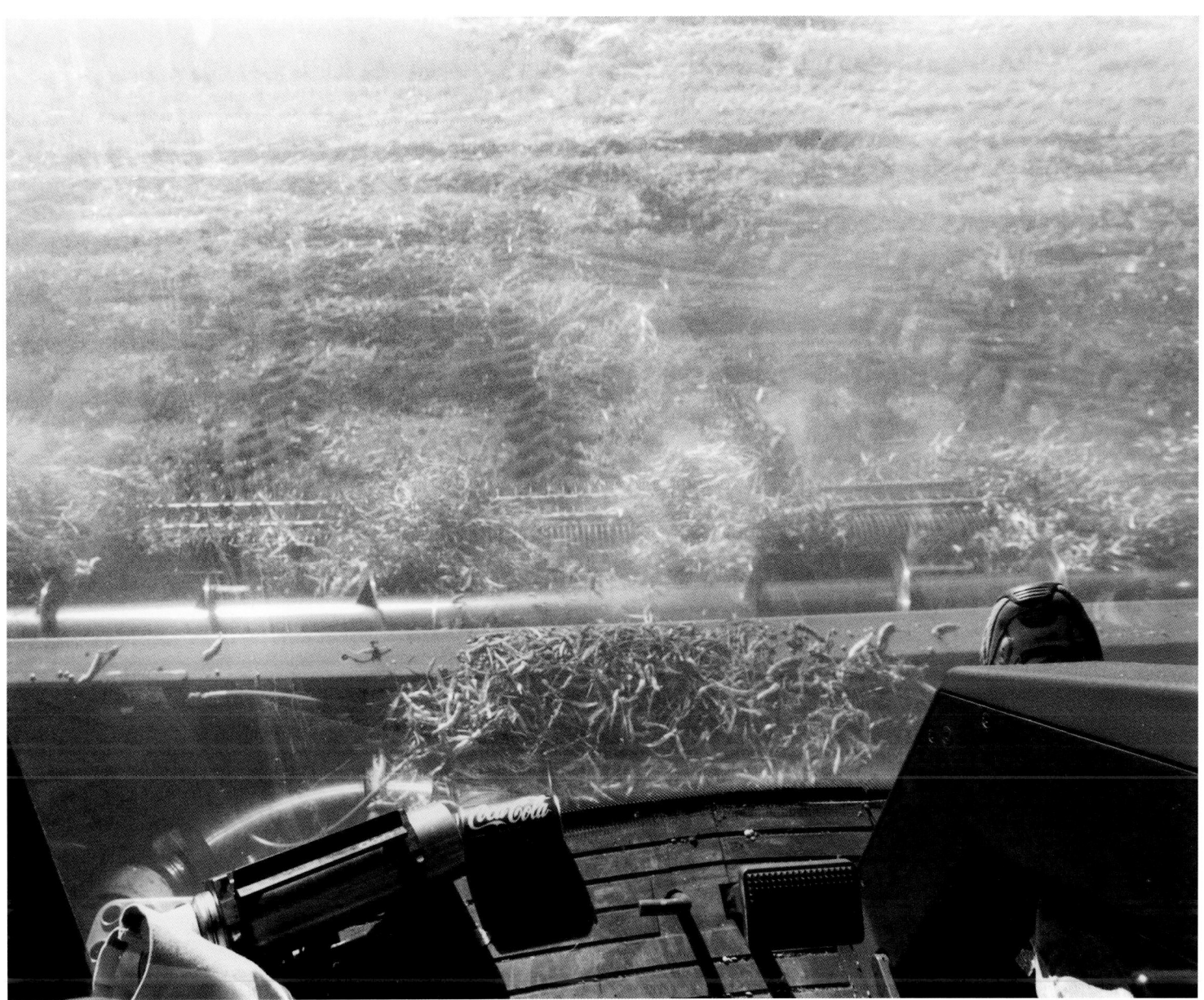

Dad, soybean harvest, 2006

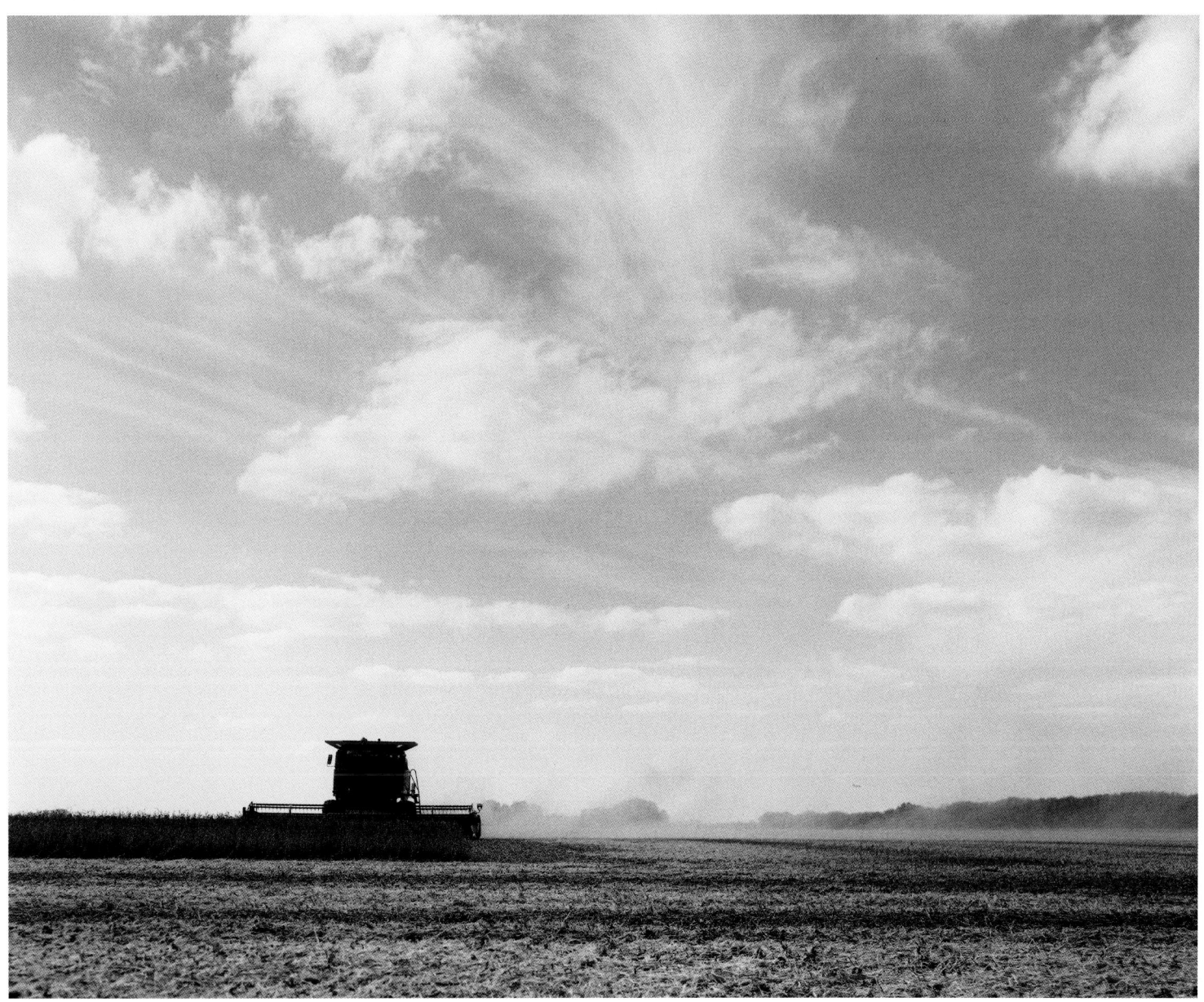

Dad combining soybeans, 2007

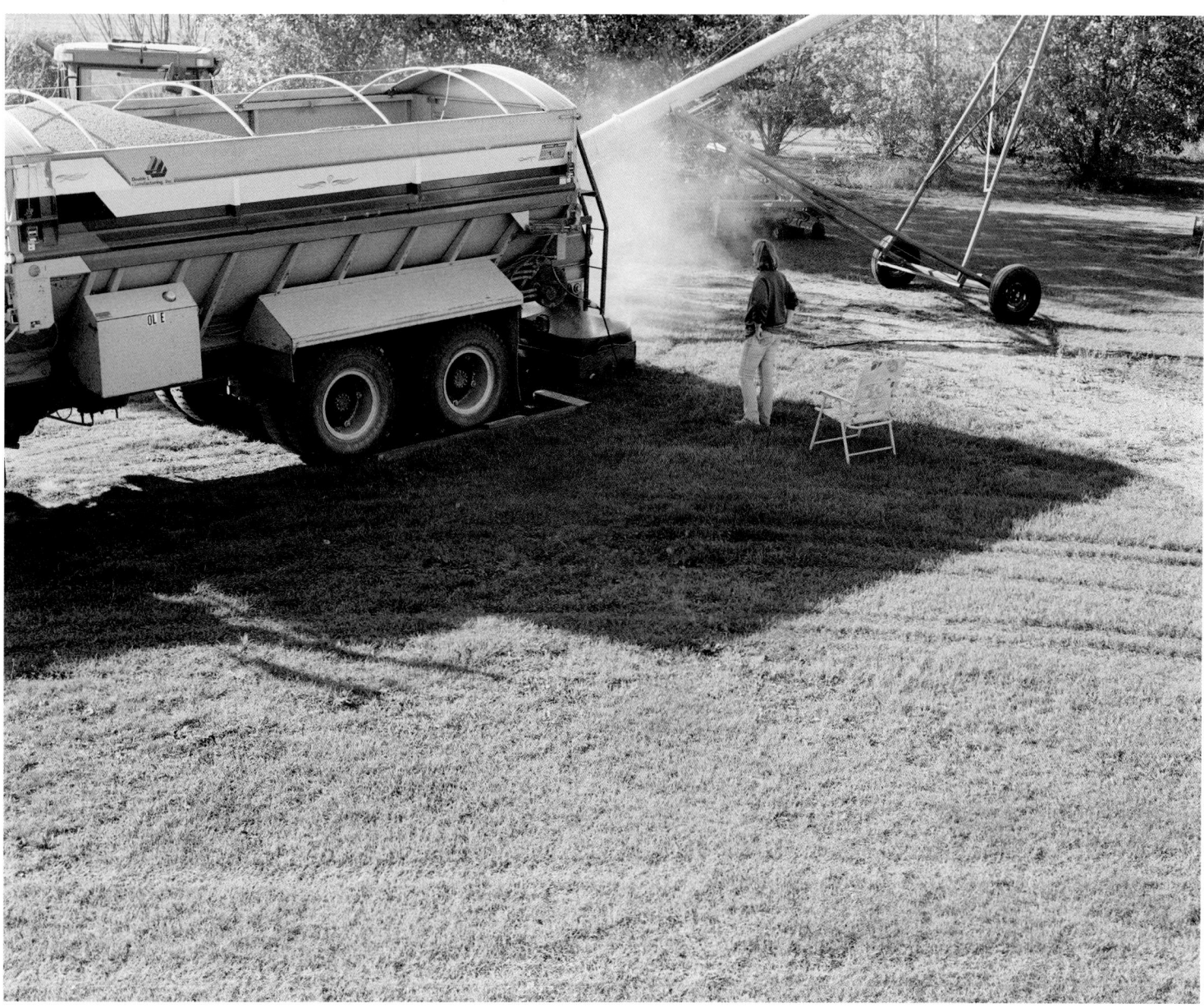

Mom storing soybeans at home, 2008

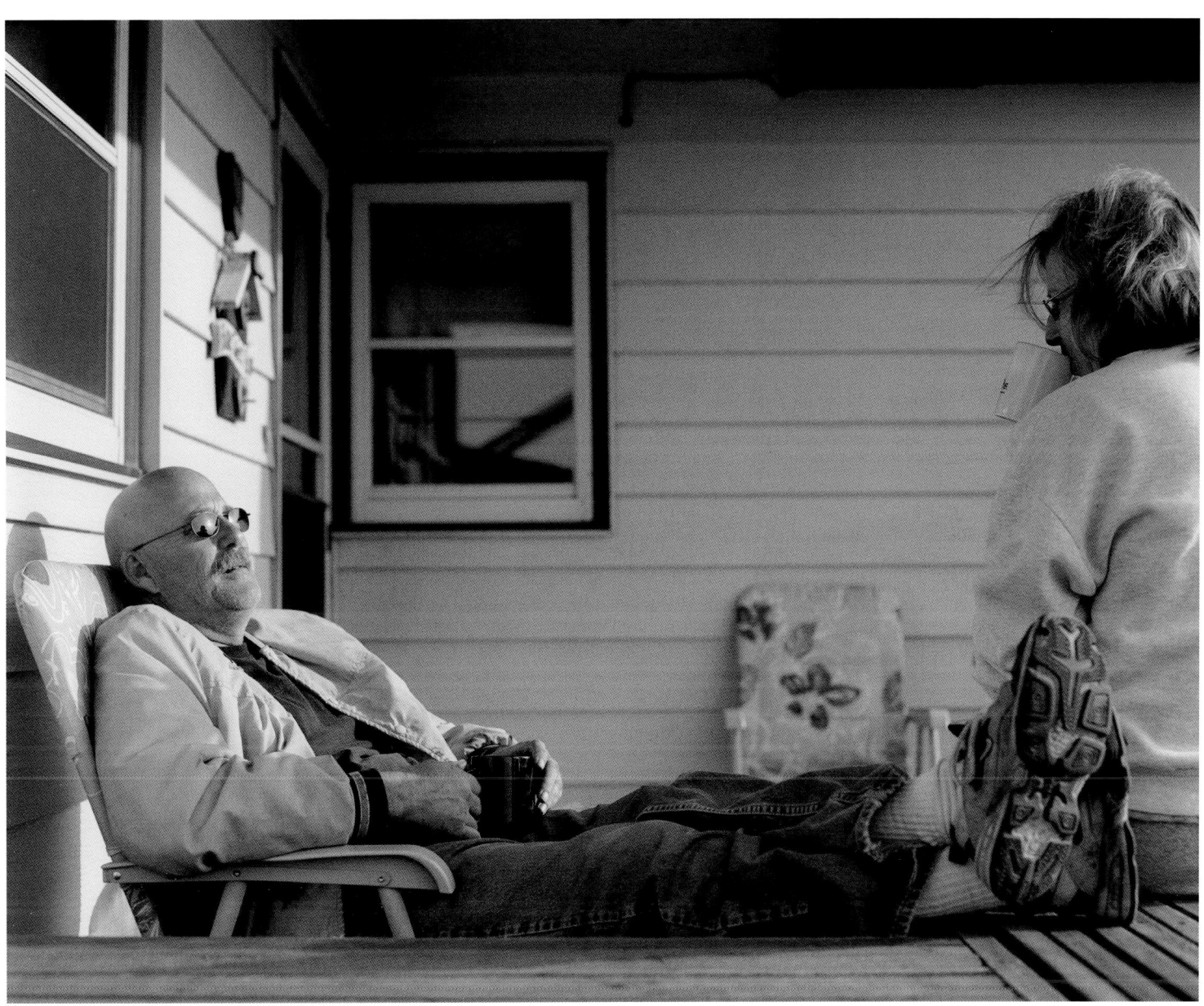

Coffee break, 2007

7:51 p.m., Christianson farm, October 2008

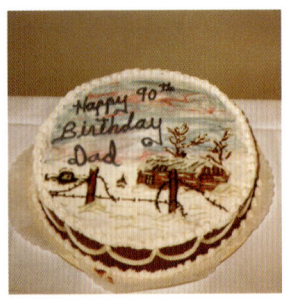
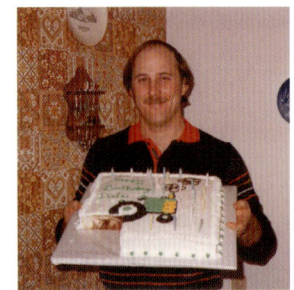
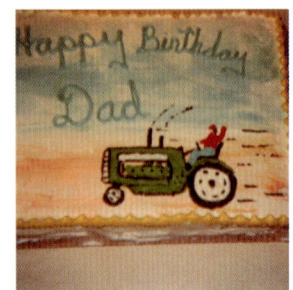
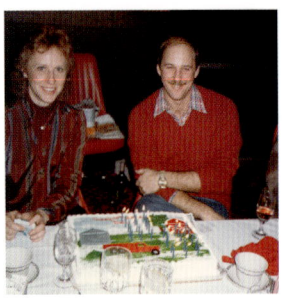
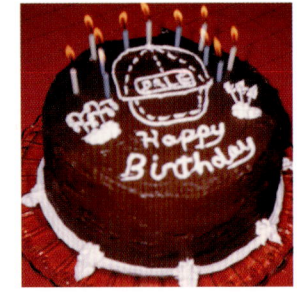
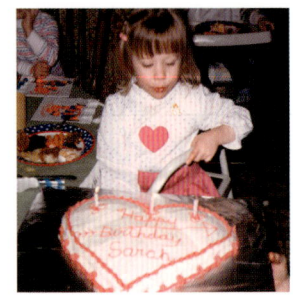
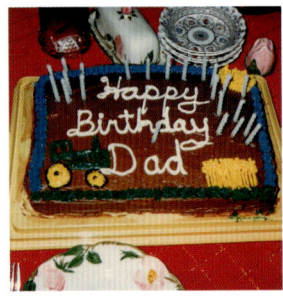
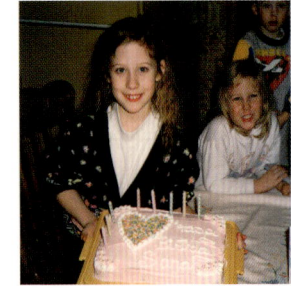
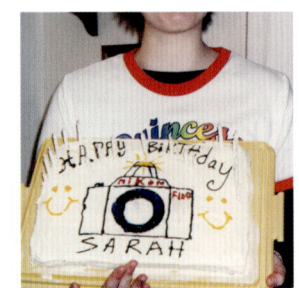

Birthday cakes, 1980–2002

FROM TRACTOR TO CAMERA

By 2006, my perception of the farm changed. I had always considered it a steady and constant place, as changeless as the granite boulders along the peripheries of our fields. Suddenly everything seemed to be in flux. My grandpa Everett—who worked on the farm until he was hospitalized—died at the age of 82. My parents burned down all the buildings on the homestead land in Bloomfield Township, including Grandpa's childhood home. They said the abandoned buildings were too much of a liability and the land would be better used as a field again. Grandma Margaret sold her farmhouse and moved to town. She and Grandpa Everett had lived in it during their married life; it had been her own grandparents' home 100 years before. I moved to Minneapolis to start graduate school. My sister moved to Fargo to work as a hair stylist, and my brother moved to a suburb in the Twin Cities to restore classic cars. I came to the realization that my parents would probably be the last of four consecutive generations of Christiansons to farm our land.

This was my impetus to document our farm, reconcile its history with its uncertain future, and explore my relationship to this place.

The upper Midwest can be easily overlooked. Life there moves at a slower pace. Summers are just long enough for the growing season before winter takes hold again. The topography is endlessly flat and presumably monotonous. However, for myself and others who have spent our lives there, the landscape is less vast than it is intimate: stories unfold with every farmstead, windbreak, landmark, and field.

Long ago, when parchment and vellum were scarce, these manuscript pages were scraped clean of text to be used over and over. The underwriting of the previous layers inevitably showed through and intermingled with the new text, creating a palimpsest. The land is a palimpsest. The history of our farm is marked again and again in the soil each season. This idea extends to other aspects of our history: the recording of our heights on a closet door, Great-grandma Claire's 5-year-diary entries, and the faint signature of my great-great-grandfather on the wall of a barn in Norway.

Like my ancestors, I left my home in search of love and better opportunities for work. I return to North Dakota, as on a pilgrimage, because the place haunts my dreams. I am compelled to photograph there and to share this familial landscape with others. No matter where I live, the farm will always be my center, my homeplace.

Sarah Christianson, San Francisco, CA
February 2013

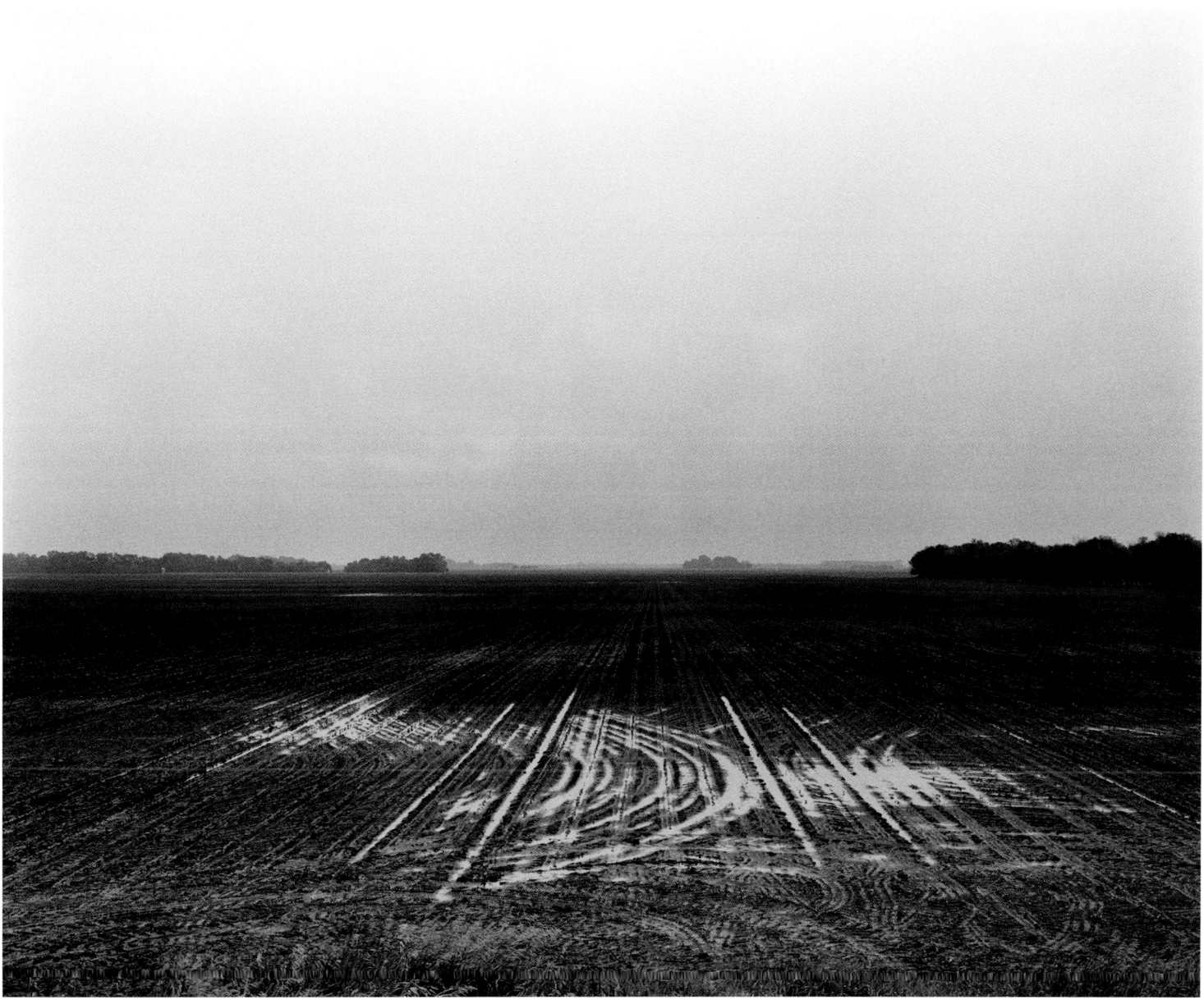

Section 23, 2007

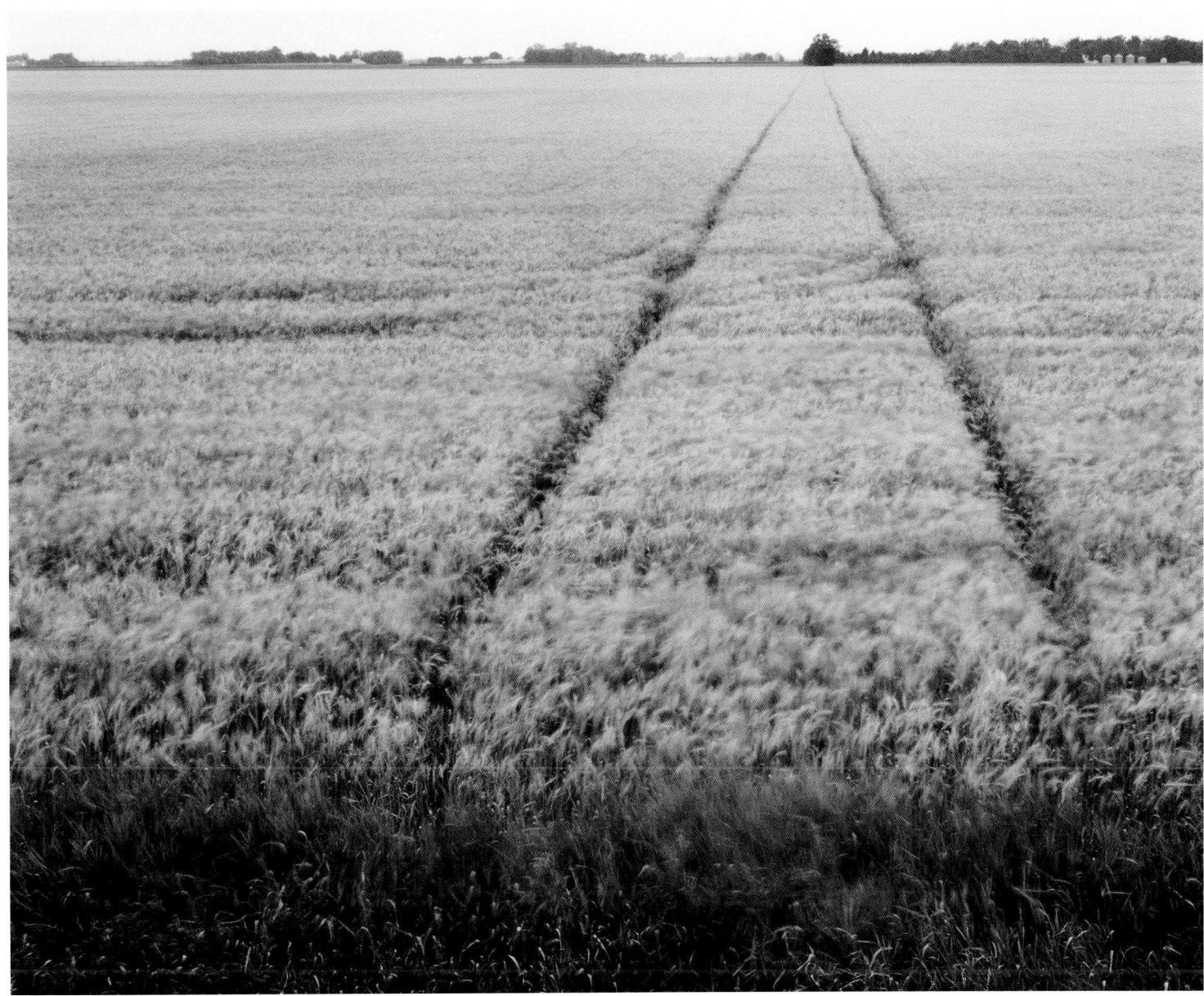

Soilbank, 2007

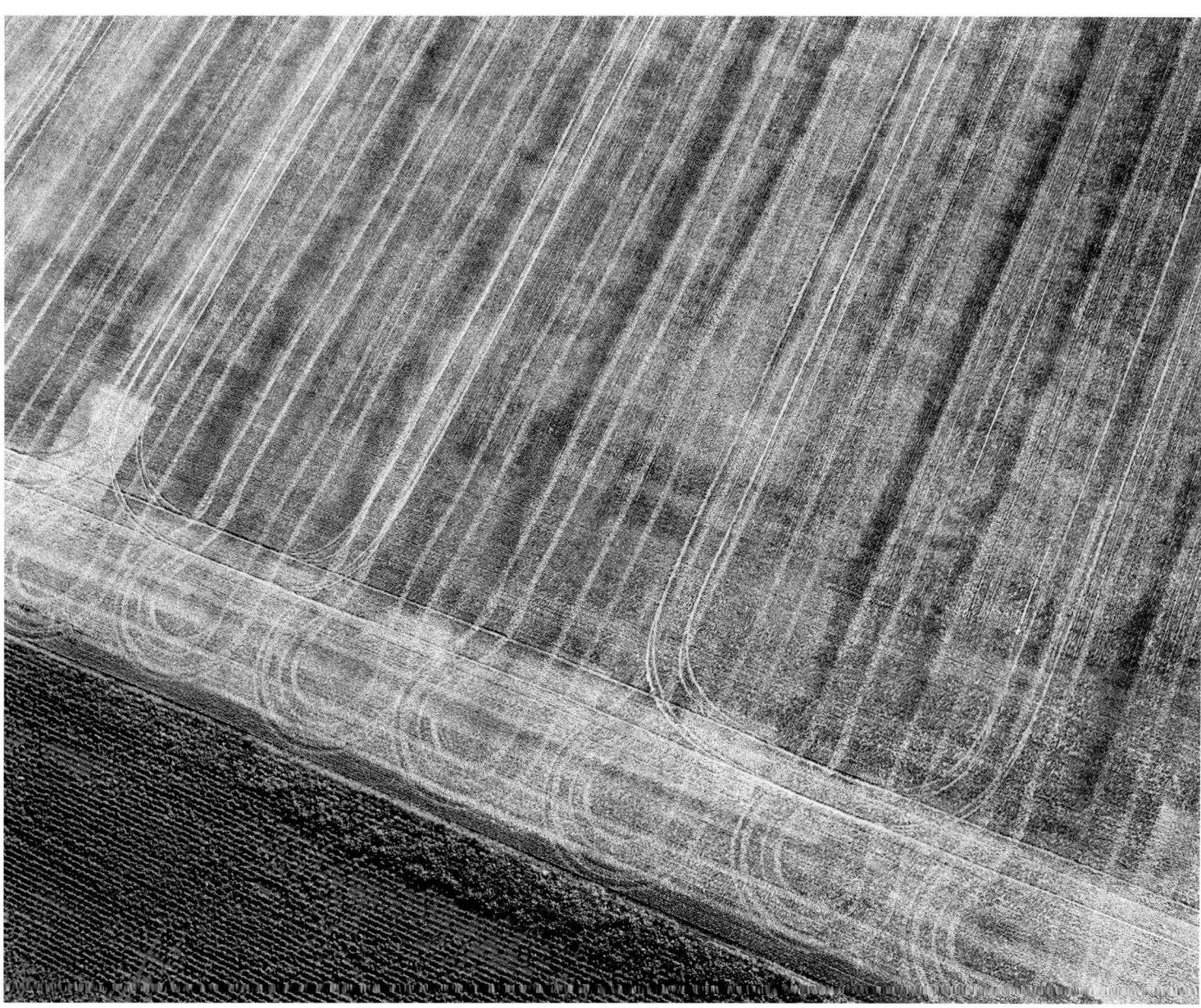

Traces, 2007

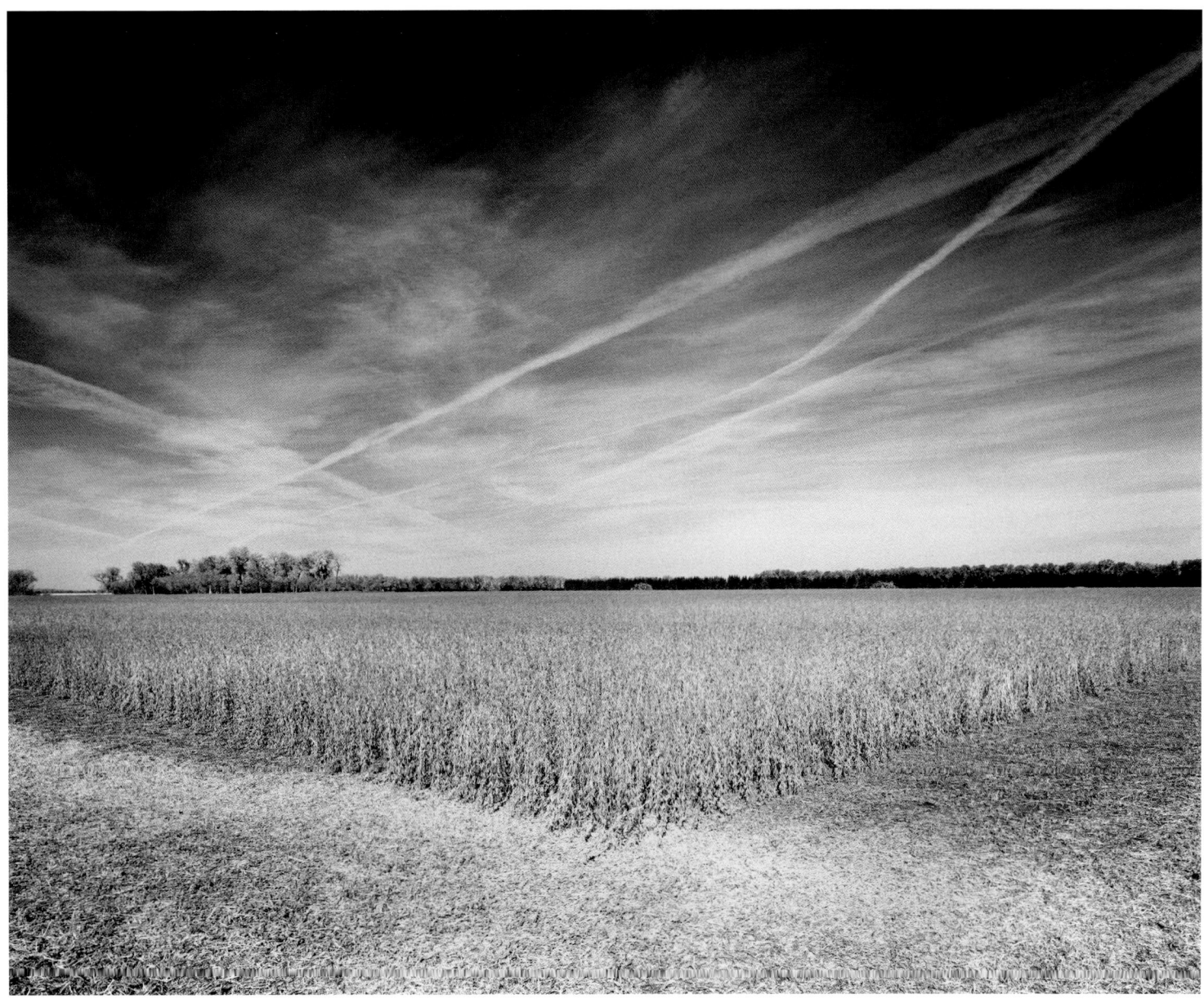

Soybeans, Tree Claim, 2007

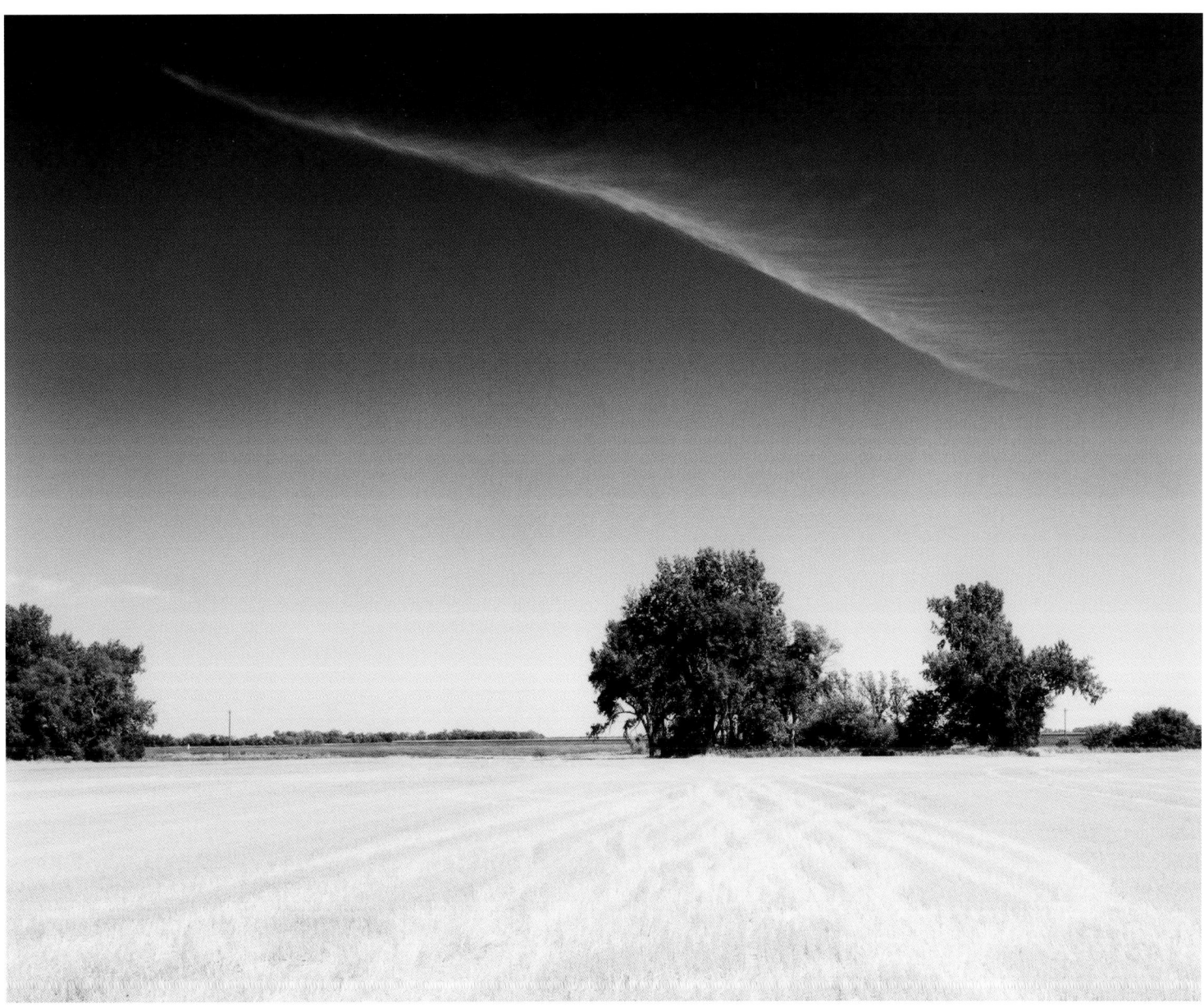

Homestead, 2007

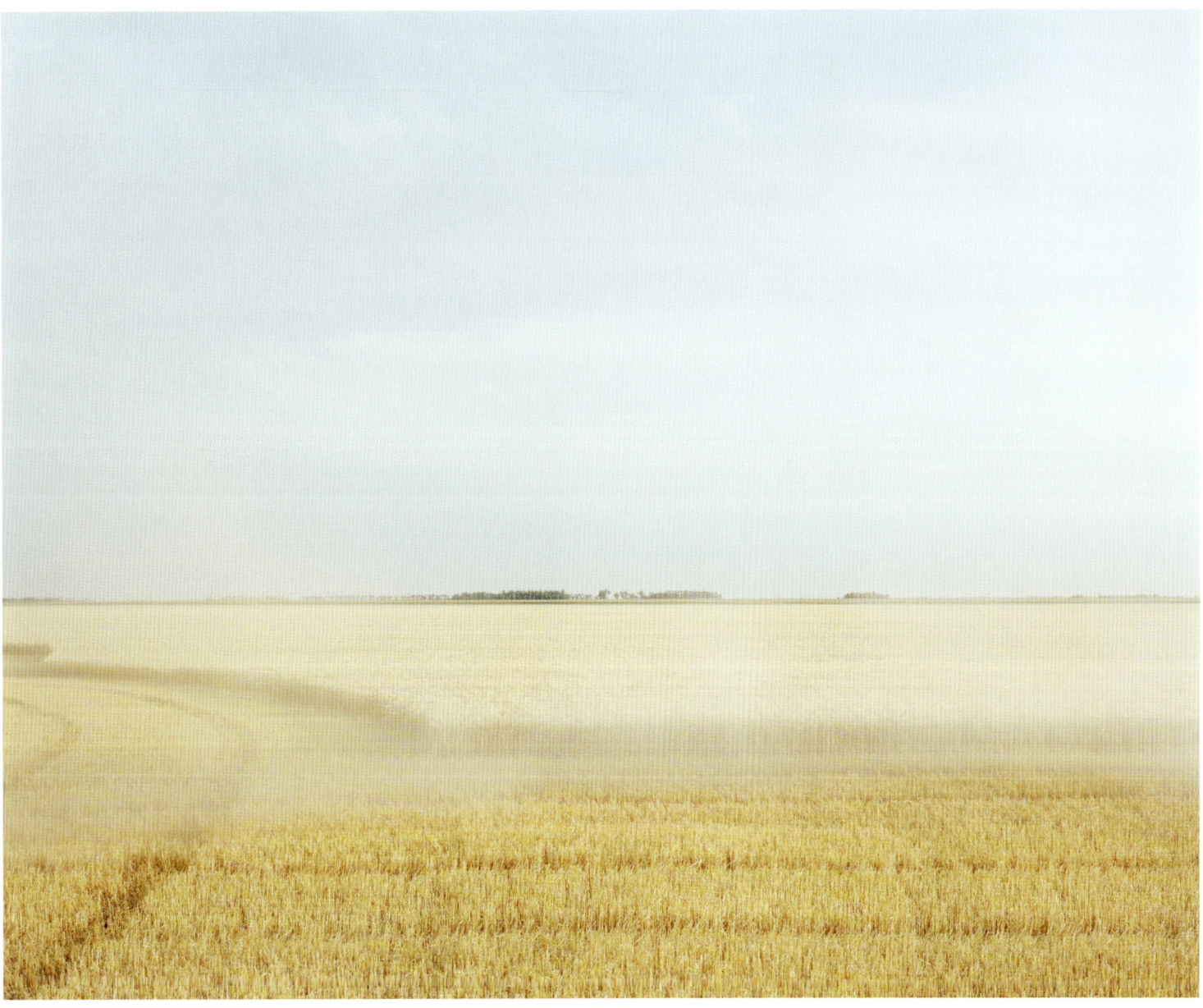

Wheat harvest, 2007

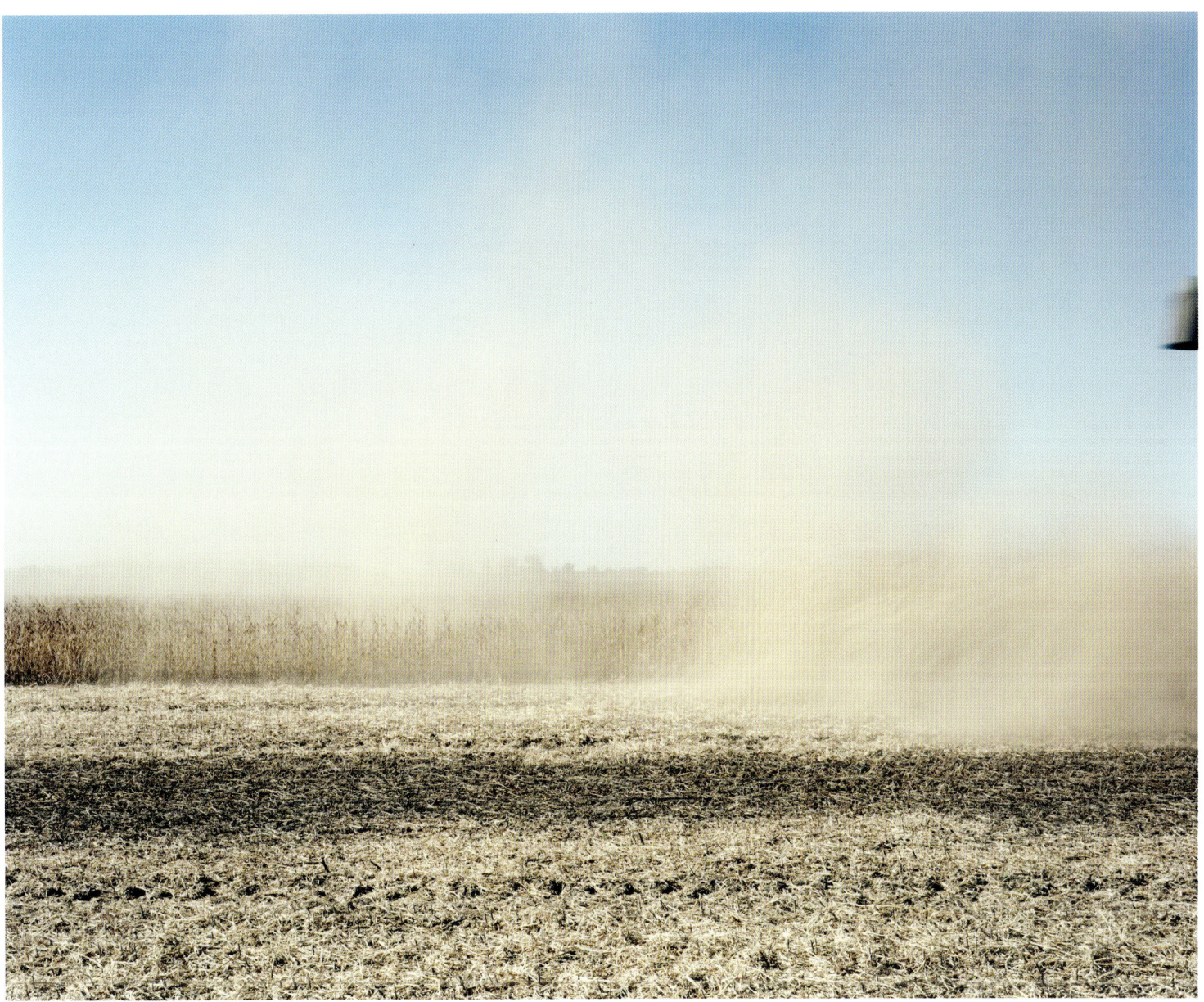

Soybean harvest, 2008

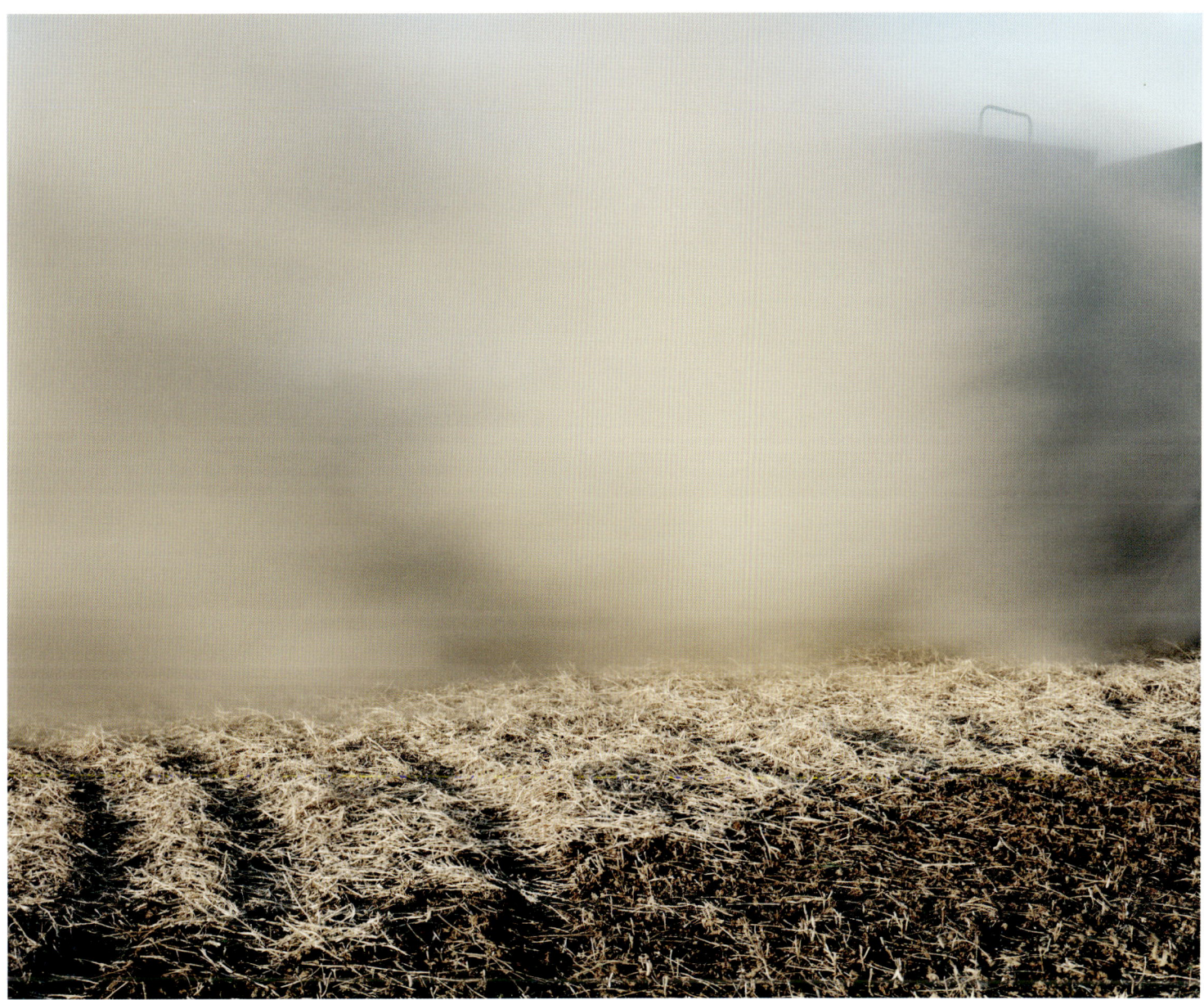

Soybean harvest, 2008

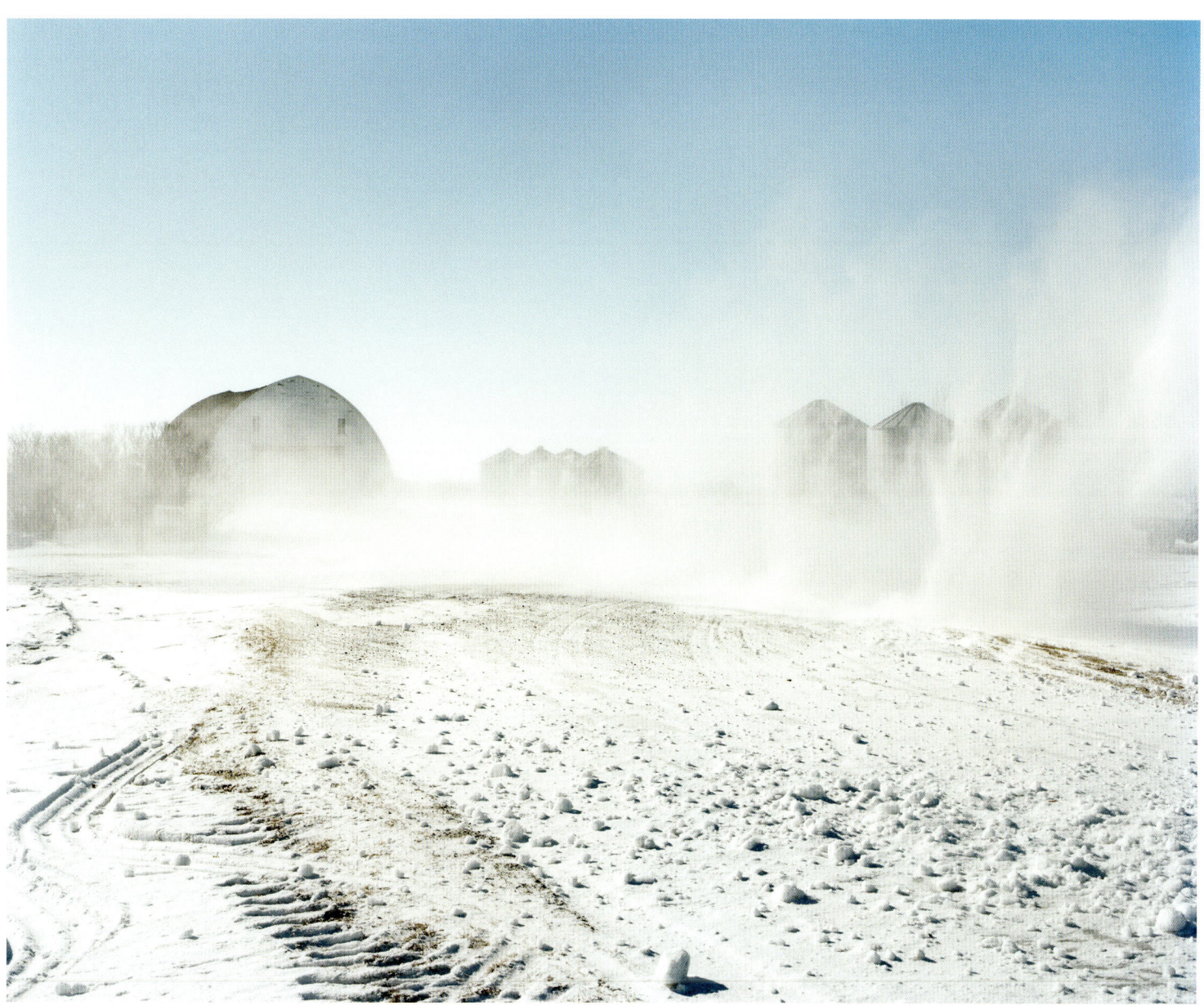

Driveway, 2009

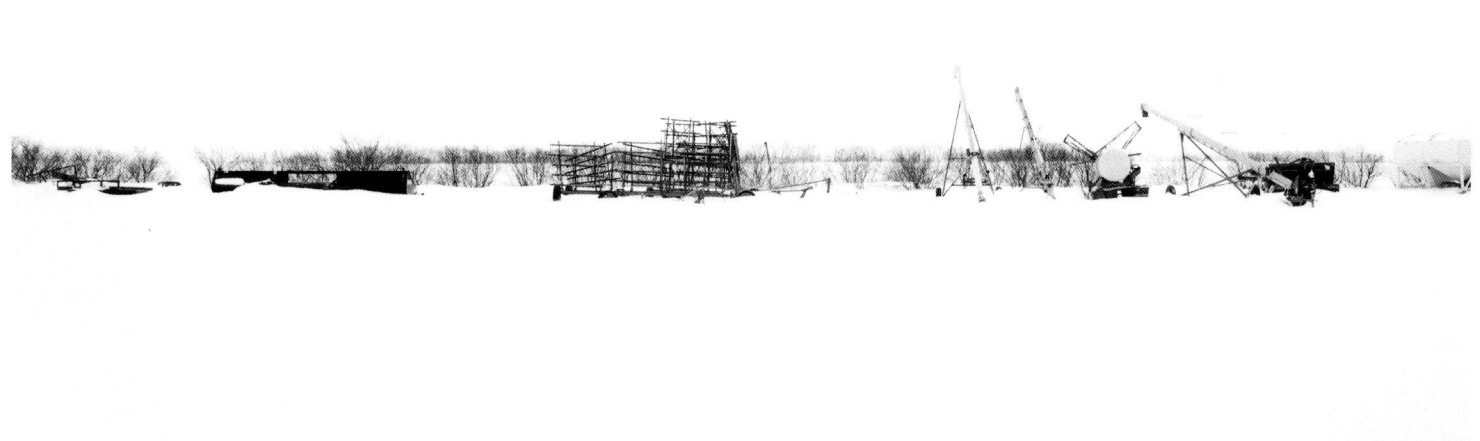

Equipment, 2008

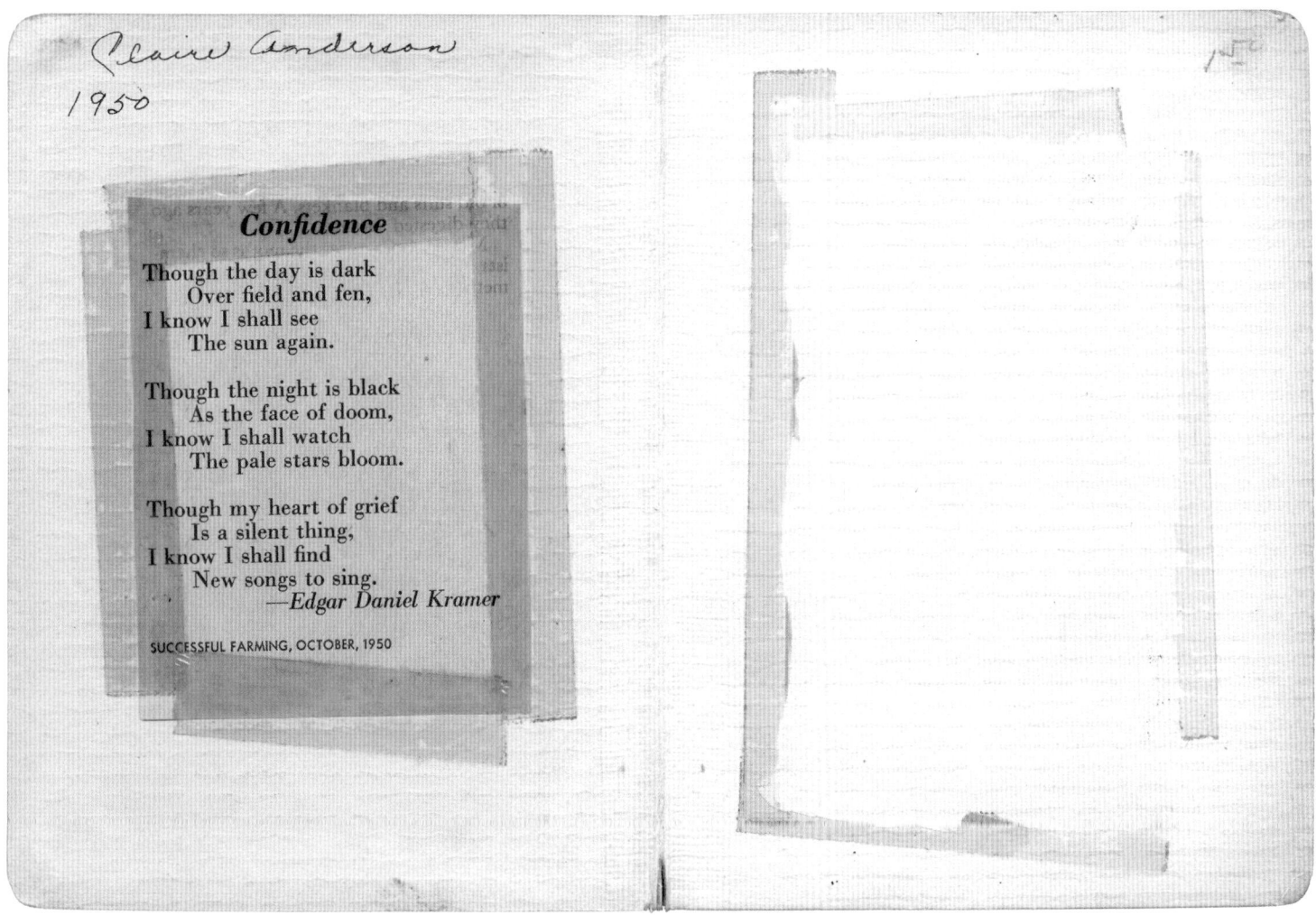

Claire Anderson

1950

Confidence

Though the day is dark
    Over field and fen,
I know I shall see
    The sun again.

Though the night is black
    As the face of doom,
I know I shall watch
    The pale stars bloom.

Though my heart of grief
    Is a silent thing,
I know I shall find
    New songs to sing.
      —*Edgar Daniel Kramer*

SUCCESSFUL FARMING, OCTOBER, 1950

Poem, Great-grandma Claire's diary, 1950

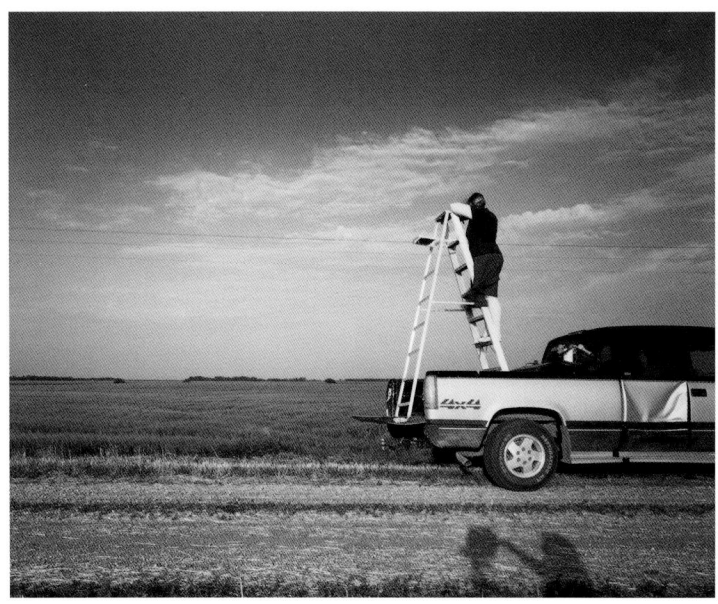

Self-portrait with Grandma Margaret's help, 2008

ACKNOWLEDGMENTS

This book is dedicated to my family: for supporting me, humoring me, and allowing me to document our story. I would especially like to thank my grandparents, Margaret and Everett Christianson, for laying down the foundation for this project through their genealogy research, travels, and preservation of family materials. And my husband, Jesse Mullan, for his constant encouragement and help with articulating and editing the work.

Many other organizations and individuals have made this project possible. I would also like to thank:

The University of Minnesota's Office of International Programs, for the Walter H. Judd Graduate and Professional Fellowship that enabled me to travel and photograph the farms throughout Norway.

All of the families there that graciously let me roam around their properties with my camera, unannounced and unable to speak a word of Norwegian.

My distant Norwegian relatives, the Holters and Kvæls, for reestablishing our family connections and hosting me.

Arnold Alanen, for the eloquent introduction he wrote after discovering many similarities in our personal histories.

Michael Itkoff and Taj Forer, for recognizing the potential of this project.

Chandler O'Leary, for being my champion, cheerleader, and wordsmith since the very beginning.

And finally, Paul Armstrong; Central Valley Bean Coop (Gary Fuglesten, Manager); Dale and Rose Christianson; Margaret Christianson; Jesse Mullan; Chad, Allison, Grace, and Anna Norgard; Richard Norgard; Kristen Peters and Christopher Webster; RayKo Photo Center; Jens A. Tkotz; and Jay Tyrrell, for their generous contributions toward the publishing of this book.